Framework For Life

The Path Among the Maze

Sharath K Bhaskaran

DEDICATION

To the quiet architects of their own becoming—
Those who chose the harder path not for glory,
But because it was true.
To the seekers who refused to be numbed by comfort,
Who traded distraction for depth,
And chose to bear the solitude that clarity demands.
To the doers who build not for applause,
But to leave behind something real—
A bridge, a book, a better way forward.
To every soul who's stood at the edge of the maze,
Tempted by ease but drawn by purpose,
May this serve as both compass and company.
And to the legends who came before—
Da Vinci, Lincoln, Curie, Tesla, Jobs, Buffett—
Your lives whisper a challenge:
Make it count.
— Sharath K Bhaskar

ACKNOWLEDGMENTS

This book is a path traced through complexity—not toward certainty, but toward clarity. It stands on the shoulders of those who lived deliberately, questioned deeply, built persistently, and illuminated the many ways we can walk through life with meaning and integrity. To Leonardo da Vinci, whose endless curiosity met focused mastery in the anatomy of both nature and invention. To Abraham Lincoln, who anchored liberty in a sea of chaos and showed us how moral courage can steady a nation. To Thomas Edison, who turned failure into fuel and progress into practice. To Ludwig van Beethoven, whose deafness became not a limitation but a boundary that sharpened his genius. To Marie Curie, whose commitment to knowledge withstood both exclusion and exhaustion. To Rosa Parks, who revealed that stillness, too, can be a form of fire. To Oscar Wilde, whose pursuit of beauty and pleasure ultimately unveiled the spiritual cost of chasing surface over substance. To Steve Jobs, who forged the self not through comfort, but through the act of creating the future. To Nikola Tesla, whose focused solitude and uncompromising will helped wire the modern world. To Warren Buffett, who taught us that wisdom often whispers, that compounding—whether in wealth or growth—is built on patience and principle. And to Carl Jung, whose exploration of the psyche offered a mirror to the soul—reminding us that we become whole not by perfection, but by integration. Their stories are not references; they are guideposts. This book is for those brave enough to walk. — Sharath K Bhaskaran

CONTENTS

1 THE MAZE OF TOO MANY OPTIONS
The Illusion of Endless Trails

Picture yourself standing on a vast, rolling plain. There are no walls, no fences, no signs. Only hills and valleys stretching in every direction, as far as the eye can see. Some paths are faint and winding, like trails forged by uncertain wanderers. Others are wide and well-trodden. Many simply fade into wild grasses. Above you, the sky is wide and limitless. Behind you, the world you've outgrown. Ahead? Everything. And nothing.

You are told: "Walk wherever you wish. This is freedom."

And for a moment, it feels like liberation. There is no map, no authority dictating direction. You are free to explore, to run, to roam.

But time passes. The sun moves. And you haven't moved. You're still scanning the horizon, turning in circles, unsure which trail to take. With each new option you spot, the last feels less certain. What if you walk too far in one direction and regret it? What if the most beautiful trail is the one just over the next hill? What if... you never find your "true" path?

In this meadow of endless possibility, your feet remain still.

And so it begins: not a crisis of restriction, but of abundance.

The Tyranny of Infinite Possibility

Barry Schwartz, in his work on the *paradox of choice*, describes how abundance can undermine satisfaction. This is not merely about shopping. It is existential. The more choices you have, the more pressure you feel to choose perfectly—and the more acute your fear of choosing wrong.

Each unopened door becomes a ghost of possibility. Each path not taken a version of you unlived. The moment you commit, you kill off infinite alternatives. And so, we hover. We hesitate. We tinker with possibility like a painter eternally mixing colors but never touching canvas.

This paralysis—this suspension in a liminal space between intention and action—can wear the appearance of productivity. We research more, compare more, plan longer. But beneath it lies a quiet dread: that we are not making progress, we are stalling. Every delay hides the hope that the "perfect" door will one day announce itself, shining and obvious, risk-free and regret-proof.

But perfection is a myth, and delay is not neutral—it's costly.

Opportunity Cost: The Price of Waiting

Every choice has a price, and often, the steepest price is not what we pay to choose, but what we forfeit by not choosing.

Economists call this *opportunity cost*: the value of the best alternative you gave up. But in life, this cost isn't just monetary—it's spiritual, emotional, and temporal. Every moment spent not committing to a direction is a moment not spent growing in that direction. While you weigh your options, the world moves forward. And while freedom feels like floating above the fray, in reality, time is always choosing for you.

You miss friendships that could have deepened. Skills that could have matured. Careers that could have been meaningful. Lives that could have been lived.

The hallway feels infinite, but your time in it is not.

The Mirage of the Reversible Path

Modern life whispers a seductive promise: "Don't worry, you can always come back. You can always start again." And yes, we have more mobility and reboots than ever before.

But not immunity from time.

Every year shapes us—our energy, our responsibilities, our relationships. And some trails—like certain passions, places, or callings—are more easily walked at 25 than at 65. Flexibility is real. But so is entropy.

And so, waiting for the "right" path can become its own form of wandering. A long, slow loop in the tall grass that leads back to the same place.

The Wisdom of the Walker

Now imagine two travellers.

One picks a direction. Perhaps arbitrarily. She walks. She encounters hills, brambles, weather, forks. But with each step, her legs strengthen. She learns how to read the land. She discovers what kind of terrain suits her. Maybe she even changes course—but now she does so with experience, not theory.

The other stands still. He surveys. He sketches maps in his mind. He fears making the wrong choice. Years pass. The sky changes color. But he remains in place, consumed by the possibility of perfection.

Which traveller, you might ask, is more free?

Clarity Comes After, Not Before

One of the cruel tricks our minds play is demanding clarity before action—requiring certainty before committing. But clarity is not a prerequisite for movement. It is the fruit of movement.

You do not discover your path fully in theory. You discover it by walking.

Think of the sculptor who begins with a block of marble. He doesn't wait to see the full figure in his mind before striking. Each cut reveals. Each chisel is an act of faith, of creation. So it is with life. We carve ourselves out of our actions.

Fear is a Signpost, Not a Stop Sign

The fear of choosing is real: fear of regret, of failure, of missing out. But these are not good reasons to stall. They are signs that something meaningful is at stake. Fear is the shadow cast by a potentially meaningful choice. It points, it signals—but it should not command.

In truth, the longer you wait, the more fear grows. Action is how fear is transformed. Not avoided, but walked through. You don't wait for courage to begin—you generate courage by beginning.

The Call to Choose

Choice is not just a means of navigating life. It is how we shape life. Every great work, every great love, every great insight—was born not from endless deliberation, but from a decision to begin.

So choose.

Not rashly, but resolutely. Not because the door is perfect, but because it is real. Because life is not waiting behind the next door—it's waiting on the other side of *any* door you dare to walk through.

You are not trapped in this maze. You are simply unclaimed. And the act of claiming yourself begins with a step.

Choose not to drift. Choose not to stall. Choose, not because you know everything—but because movement itself is sacred.

The Truth Hidden in the Maze

What the maze never tells you is this: you are not just here to find the perfect turn.
You are here to move—step by step—and build a life within its winding paths.

The crossroads, dead ends, and hidden passages are not traps. They are invitations.
The life you're seeking isn't waiting at some final destination—it's being shaped in every choice, every pivot, every stumble forward.

So walk.
Not because the path is certain, but because movement is sacred.

You are not lost in this maze.
You are simply unclaimed. And the act of claiming yourself begins with a step.

Choose not to drift. Choose not to stall.

Choose— not because you know where the maze will lead,
but because only through motion do you become the one who can walk it.

The maze is not your prison.
It is your proving ground.

And the first act of freedom is this:
Choose.

Case Study: Leonardo da Vinci
The Genius Who Wandered the Maze

Case Study: Leonardo da Vinci
The Genius Who Wandered the Maze

In a small Tuscan town in the spring of 1452, a boy was born outside the bounds of legitimacy. He had no formal surname, no inherited status, no preordained profession. His father was a respected notary; his mother a peasant woman. From birth, Leonardo was placed in a liminal space—not quite noble, not quite common, not bound to any one path. That ambiguity, it turns out, would become the defining feature of his life.

Leonardo grew up surrounded by fields and streams, trees and animals. His earliest education came not from books but from nature itself. He observed the flight of birds, the ripple of water, the anatomy of plants. Where others saw landscape, he saw systems. Where others accepted the sky as blue, he wondered why. His curiosity was not casual—it was ravenous.

He began drawing young, and never stopped. What started as sketches of his surroundings soon became diagrams, designs, and impossible machines. But this was no idle doodling. From the beginning, Leonardo saw art as a way of understanding life, not merely representing it. Every line of his pen was a question: How does this work? What lies beneath the surface?

By the time he reached his teenage years, his father recognized his talent and arranged for him to apprentice under Andrea del Verrocchio, one of Florence's master artists. In Verrocchio's studio, Leonardo was exposed to the full spectrum of Renaissance craft: painting, sculpting, metallurgy, carpentry, drafting, mechanics. Each discipline opened a new door—and Leonardo walked through all of them.

Most apprentices aimed to master a single trade. Leonardo, however, would not be contained. He didn't want to just paint a horse; he wanted to understand the tendons beneath its skin, the way its hooves struck the earth, the mechanics of its gait. He didn't want to design a machine; he wanted to grasp the laws of motion, pressure, friction, and wind. For him, every question generated more questions. And with each answer, another door appeared.

This, perhaps, is where his great gift began to blur into burden.

Leonardo soon struck out on his own, and Florence welcomed him as a rising star. Commissions came in. Patrons lined up. He began works like The Adoration of the Magi and Saint Jerome in the Wilderness—

paintings filled with breathtaking energy and insight. Yet, they remained unfinished. He would begin with fire, sketching dozens of studies, innovating techniques, inventing compositions. But then... the energy would shift. A new idea would appear. A new concept. A more interesting question. The hallway of choices stretched on.

By his late 30s, he moved to Milan to serve the Duke Ludovico Sforza—not just as a painter, but as a military engineer, architect, and court entertainer. Here again, the maze expanded. He designed weapons of war he hoped would never be used. He studied city planning, canals, fortresses, hydraulic systems. He dissected human corpses at night and filled notebooks with anatomical observations centuries ahead of modern medicine. He drafted elaborate treatises on flight, light, mechanics, painting, and the structure of the human body.

Yet again, very little was completed.

For nearly 17 years in Milan, Leonardo produced only a handful of finished works. The most notable was The Last Supper, and even it began as an experiment in technique that quickly decayed due to his unconventional materials. Still, the painting remains one of the most iconic in history—an emotional symphony frozen in pigment. It proves what Leonardo could do when he committed, however briefly, to completion.

But these moments were exceptions, not the rule.

As the years passed, his projects grew more ambitious, and his list of unfinished works longer. He began designing an equestrian statue for the Duke—a massive bronze horse that would be the largest in the world. He studied horses obsessively, drawing dozens of dynamic studies, developing complex casting methods. But the bronze was repurposed for cannons. The project was abandoned.

And still, Leonardo kept recording. His notebooks, now numbering thousands of pages, became labyrinths of their own—filled with mirrored handwriting, sketches, diagrams, mechanical dreams, philosophical musings, grocery lists, and cryptic reminders. He wrote backwards, as if protecting the ideas from easy consumption. Or perhaps from judgment.

He once began a treatise on painting, promising to elevate the art from craft to science. Another on anatomy. Another on flight. None were completed. In one margin he scribbled, almost as a confession: "Tell me if anything was ever done."

This was not the cry of a man who had done nothing. It was the ache of a man who had done almost everything—but always just shy of the finish line.

As he aged, his fame did not fade. He returned to Florence, clashed with Michelangelo, and worked for Cesare Borgia as a military advisor. He sketched urban sanitation plans, designed ideal cities, and studied the flow of rivers. Later, in Rome, he worked under the patronage of Pope Leo X. But again, commissions were rare. His reputation was that of a genius, yes—but an unreliable one. A visionary who would start anything, but finish almost nothing.

It was in France, in the final years of his life, that Leonardo found a kind of peace. King Francis I invited him to the Château du Clos Lucé, where he was given comfort, respect, and freedom. He brought with him a lion-shaped automaton, dozens of paintings (including the Mona Lisa), and trunks of notebooks—his real legacy.

By then, he was mostly paralyzed in his right hand. He wrote with difficulty. But the thoughts never stopped. He still dreamed of finishing his treatises, of compiling his discoveries, of bringing order to the mental chaos he had spent decades unleashing. But time had caught up.

He died in 1519 at age 67, honored and beloved, yet still murmuring regrets. According to legend, he claimed he had "offended God and mankind by not having worked at his art as he should have." Whether he truly said it or not, the feeling rings true.

Leonardo's life, then, becomes something more than the myth of the polymath. It becomes a mirror for modern man—especially those of us lost in a sea of choices.

He had more natural ability than perhaps any person in history. He was a scientist before science existed as a discipline, an engineer before the Industrial Revolution, an artist whose eyes saw into the soul. But he was also indecisive, fragmented, and plagued by perfectionism.

He could never settle on a single path, and in refusing to choose, he spread his genius wide—but thin.

And yet, even his fragments changed the world.

His notebooks influenced generations of thinkers. His anatomy sketches informed modern biology. His design for a helicopter inspired 20th-century engineers. His paintings shaped the emotional vocabulary of art forever. He didn't have to finish everything to make an indelible mark.

Still, his life raises the central question of this chapter: what might he have accomplished if he had chosen one door, and walked fully through it?

That is not to say Leonardo erred in his exploration. We owe much of our wonder to the fact that he remained a seeker. But his story offers a truth that even the most gifted among us must confront:

Infinite freedom is not infinite power.
It is a burden—unless shaped by choice.

Leonardo da Vinci shows us what brilliance looks like when it refuses to be lost—captured not in grand monuments, but in pages of ink and wonder. He may have left many works unfinished, but he did not let his thoughts vanish. He wrote them down. He sketched them, annotated them, returned to them, and preserved them. That choice—to document the maze rather than merely wander it—is what saved his genius from obscurity.

He reminds us that even when a path feels uncertain, choosing to *record the journey* can be an act of purpose. That clarity doesn't always come from completion, but from articulation. That a legacy can emerge not just from masterpieces, but from the commitment to trace what one sees, feels, and seeks.

So as you stand before your own hallway of doors—each one inviting, each one unknown—remember this: you do not need Leonardo's genius. But you can embrace his discipline of reflection.

Journal your thoughts. Capture your questions. Chronicle your wanderings.

Because even half-built bridges can lead others across if the blueprints remain.

Leonardo did not finish everything. But by choosing to *write it down*, he left behind a map—unfinished, yes, but luminous. And that map, centuries later, still guides the minds of those who dare to dream broadly and think deeply.

May his brilliance inspire you.
May his discipline instruct you.
And may his notebooks remind you that in a world of infinite doors, even a single page can become a legacy.

Here are **5 key takeaways** from the Leonardo da Vinci case study

1. Curiosity Is a Gift—But Without Direction, It Can Become a Trap

Leonardo's boundless curiosity led him to explore every field imaginable. But his unwillingness to choose a focus often left him adrift. Curiosity is powerful—but it needs a rudder to become transformative.

2. Infinite Options Create Paralysis, Not Progress

Though Leonardo had unmatched freedom to pursue any idea, this abundance of choice often paralyzed his ability to commit. His life illustrates the paradox of choice: more options don't guarantee more fulfilment—just more hesitation.

3. Starting Everything Is Not the Same as Finishing Something

Leonardo began countless projects—artworks, treatises, inventions—but completed few. While his sketches and notes are invaluable, many of his greatest ideas remained unrealized. There is a distinct power in *completion*, even over perfection.

4. Recording the Journey Is Itself a Legacy

Despite unfinished work, Leonardo's choice to meticulously document his thoughts through journaling preserved his genius for future generations. Reflection and record-keeping can transform private exploration into public contribution.

5. You Don't Need Genius to Choose—You Need Courage

Leonardo's story is not a call to be a polymath. It's a reminder that what matters most is not the scale of your potential, but the *act of choosing*. Choosing one door, one path, one purpose—however imperfect—can change everything.

2 LIBERTY WITHOUT A COMPASS

The Lost Navigator in the Sea of Freedom

There is a strange fear that lives inside freedom—one few ever name.

At first glance, liberty appears as the ultimate gift: a vast, open sea with no boundaries, no restrictions, and infinite destinations. It promises escape, possibility, and power. And yet, countless people given this freedom find themselves drifting—overwhelmed, directionless, and strangely anxious. In this sea, they are free, yes—but without a compass, they are also *lost*.

To navigate liberty, you must first know who you are. Not just what you want in a moment, but what you value—deeply, consistently, across time and circumstance. Without this internal compass, freedom becomes a void. The ship is yours, but the stars have vanished. And so, you float.

The Weight of Freedom

The modern world offers more liberty than any civilization in human history. You are free to choose your career, your city, your lifestyle, your beliefs, even your identity. But this dizzying array of choices can become a burden. When there are no clear paths, no assigned roles, no cultural scripts to follow, the pressure to define your own becomes immense.

This is the great irony of freedom: it does not remove the need for structure—it increases it.

If no one else is going to tell you who you are, then you must do it yourself. That is the price of autonomy: self-authorship. Freedom demands not just movement, but meaning. And meaning requires *values*.

What Is a Value?

A value is not a slogan, a brand, or a vibe. It is not whatever is currently trending on your feed or the latest belief adopted by your peer group. A value is a deeply held principle that helps you *filter* the world—an inner standard against which all decisions are weighed.

Values answer essential questions:

- What matters most?
- What do I owe others?
- What will I sacrifice for?
- What is non-negotiable, even if it's unpopular?

In the absence of such anchors, we become not free spirits, but reactionary ones—drifting from impulse to impulse, trend to trend, cause to cause. We respond, but we do not *choose*.

The Difference Between Direction and Drift

Imagine two ships at sea. One has a compass, a map, and a destination. It adjusts for wind, reroutes around storms, but always moves with purpose. The second ship is equipped with every luxury and technological advance—but no compass. It moves rapidly, even beautifully, but in circles. Its motion disguises its aimlessness.

The first ship may face setbacks, but it knows where it's going. The second ship may feel exhilarating, but it ultimately goes nowhere.

Many people live as the second ship. They believe they are exercising freedom by keeping every option open, rejecting all structure, and constantly reinventing themselves. But in truth, they are lost navigators—refusing to commit to direction, confusing *freedom from* with *freedom for*.

Freedom from constraint is only the beginning. To live meaningfully, you must decide what your freedom is *for*.

Popular Isn't Permanent

In a world saturated with information and performance, values are often replaced with signals. People adopt the slogans of the moment— "Live your truth," "Do what feels good," "No one can tell you who to be"—as if these are deep truths rather than transient mantras.

These messages sound empowering, but they often fail us in the moments that matter most. When you are betrayed by a friend, lied to by a leader, broken by grief, tempted by power, or confronted by injustice—pop slogans will not hold the weight of your soul. You will need something stronger. You will need values that endure beyond the mood of the moment.

Choosing values is not about branding yourself. It's about grounding yourself. The right values won't make you trendy. They'll make you trustworthy.

Finding the Compass: Knowing Yourself

So where do your values come from?

They begin with *self-awareness*. This is not some mystical concept. It means paying attention to what you feel, how you act, what haunts you, and what moves you. It means tracking patterns—what you admire in others, what you regret doing, what you're willing to fight for. It's uncomfortable work, but liberating.

Ask yourself:

- When have I felt most proud of my actions?
- What kind of behavior in others consistently earns my respect?
- What kind of behavior in myself makes me feel disgust or shame?
- What decisions have I made that I still stand by, even if they cost me?
- When did I feel most aligned—most "me"?

Patterns will emerge. Those patterns are clues to your values.

You may discover you value *honesty*, even when it's costly. Or *loyalty*, even when it's inconvenient. You may find that *freedom of thought*, *compassion for the vulnerable*, or *responsibility for your actions* are non-negotiable. These aren't inherited—they are discovered, sometimes painfully, through experience and reflection.

From Values to Decision-Making

Values are not abstract. They are tools—like a compass or sextant. They don't eliminate hard choices, but they illuminate them.

Say you value *integrity*. That single value can shape:

- What job offers you accept
- Whether you hide mistakes or admit them
- Who you trust and partner with
- Whether you follow the crowd or speak up

Or suppose you value *freedom of expression*. That will impact:

- What causes you support
- What platforms you trust
- How you handle disagreement
- What kind of environment you create for others

The stronger your values, the easier your decisions become—not because they are less complex, but because they are guided.

Without values, every decision must be made from scratch. With values, decisions align with a larger pattern. You aren't just reacting—you are *building*.

Universality Without Uniformity

But how do you know if your values are *right*?

The truth is, no value is right for everyone, everywhere. But the best values are those that **can be shared**, even across cultures, faiths, and ideologies. The human condition has patterns. We all bleed. We all love. We all long to be free and to belong.

You don't need to invent values from scratch. Across history, through philosophy, religion, literature, and everyday experience, humanity has recorded its moral experiments. We've seen what virtues uplift and what vices destroy. Now, more than ever, we can learn from cultures not our own and triangulate truths that stand the test of time.

You are not limited by where you were born. You are empowered by what you are willing to learn.

A person in Mumbai, Cairo, Berlin, or Bogotá may define "honor," "freedom," or "truth" slightly differently. But the core impulse—*to live by something that transcends appetite*—is shared. And that is where the compass can be found.

Choosing Values That Fit Your Life

A compass does not remove the storm, nor does it control the waves. What it gives you is **direction**—something to aim toward when everything else is uncertain.

Choose values that you would still hold if no one were watching. Choose values that you admire in the people you trust most. Choose values that help you become someone *you* respect.

These values should not just sound good—they should feel costly. If they never demand anything of you, they are slogans, not values.

You don't need ten. You need three to five that anchor you. They should be specific, actionable, and deeply personal:

- *I will tell the truth, even when it's uncomfortable.*
- *I will defend the dignity of others, especially when they are voiceless.*
- *I will own my mistakes and make them right.*
- *I will create, not just consume.*
- *I will live in such a way that I could explain my choices to a future child or a younger version of myself.*

These are not laws imposed by someone else. They are **chosen constraints**—boundaries that make your freedom meaningful.

From Drift to Direction

The sea of freedom is real—and you are in it. There are no buoys. No lighthouses. No assigned map. But you are not helpless. You can chart your course. And once you do, you will move—not perfectly, but purposefully.

You will begin to recognize false paths. You will know when a choice leads you closer to who you are or pulls you away from it. You will feel the subtle but powerful confidence that comes from *alignment*.

The great gift of liberty is not endless motion. It is the space to choose your values, define your path, and live it with integrity.

Don't fear the open sea. Fear being unanchored.

Choose your compass.

Point your ship.

And sail—into freedom, with direction.

Case Study: Abraham Lincoln
The Compass of Conscience

Case Study: Abraham Lincoln
The Compass of Conscience

He was born in a log cabin, obscured by the backwoods of Kentucky and Indiana. There were no maps waiting for Abraham Lincoln—no prestigious lineage, no well-paved road to greatness. His childhood offered few signposts. His family moved often. He split rails and read by firelight. In a world dominated by birthright and plantation wealth, Lincoln had little more than wit, books, and a restless hunger for understanding.

And yet, even then, something stirred in him. Not ambition in the vulgar sense, but a craving to orient his life toward *something that mattered*. He would later say, "I am nothing, but truth is everything." That early posture—humble, yet grounded in principle—would become the defining compass of his life.

As a young man, Lincoln tried many things: store clerk, postmaster, militia captain, self-taught lawyer. He was not fast to settle, not eager to perform. He was searching. And more than skills or status, he was looking for coherence. He had seen cruelty firsthand—the brutal floggings on slave farms, the casual bigotry of frontier politics—and it haunted him. Something inside refused to let it be normal. He began, quietly but relentlessly, to forge his moral compass.

He was not born into abolitionism. But he was born with *a heart that asked questions*. Why should one man own another? Why should power grant the right to dehumanize? Why does freedom apply to some but not all?

He did not answer these questions with slogans or party lines. He answered them with values.

He read the Declaration of Independence not as an artifact of rebellion, but as a promise of principle. "All men are created equal"—those words, to Lincoln, were not mere poetry. They were sacred coordinates. They gave direction not just to a nation, but to a life.

Lincoln was surrounded by men more polished, more confident, more extreme. The abolitionists called him too slow. The slaveholders called him dangerous. Many in Washington called him weak. But Lincoln had something they lacked: *a compass that did not spin with the weather*.

He did not chase popularity. He did not obey ideology. He obeyed *conscience*.

And conscience—real conscience—is slow. It weighs. It studies. It struggles. But it endures. And it *chooses*.

As President, Lincoln's world split open. The Civil War was not just a war of territory, but of truth. Could a nation truly devoted to liberty survive its betrayal in slavery? Could unity be purchased at the price of ignoring injustice?

It would have been easier to compromise, to delay, to preserve the shell of the Union at the cost of its soul. But Lincoln's compass was clear. The nation must be made whole, and slavery must end. "A house divided against itself cannot stand." This was not a tactical line—it was a moral one.

He did not relish conflict. He mourned the bloodshed. He agonized over each death. But he did not flinch from purpose. Because he had already decided, years earlier, what he stood for. And once you know your direction, you can move through storms that would sink others.

His values were not borrowed. They were built. Through poverty, through legal cases, through friendships and losses, Lincoln did the internal work of discerning what mattered. And when the time came to act, he was ready.

The Emancipation Proclamation was not just an executive order. It was the alignment of principle with power. It was liberty with a compass— freedom not as abstraction, but as action.

Even in victory, Lincoln did not gloat. He spoke not of punishment, but of healing. "With malice toward none, with charity for all..." These were not just words. They were reflections of a man who had refused to be poisoned by his enemies, because his compass pointed toward *justice* and *mercy*, not vengeance.

Then, just days after the war ended, he was gone. A bullet stopped the man—but not the movement.

What remains is not just a legacy of legislation. It is an example. The example of a man who *chose* his values, long before they were popular, long before they were safe—and let those values guide him across a landscape of chaos and war.

Lincoln teaches us that liberty without values is drift. That principle is not rigidity—it is direction. That knowing what you stand for does not make life easier, but it makes life meaningful.

And in an age where noise reigns and signals constantly shift, his life stands like a lighthouse—quiet, steady, unmistakable.

You do not need Lincoln's stature. But you need what he had: a moral compass. One forged not in comfort, but in conflict. Not imposed from above, but cultivated from within.

Your freedom is real. But so is the storm.

Choose your direction.

Let your values steer you.

And walk—not just freely, but truly.

Here are **5 key takeaways** from Abraham Lincoln's case study, tailored to the theme of Chapter 2 — *Liberty Without a Compass*:

1. **True freedom requires self-knowledge and moral clarity.** Lincoln's journey began not with external success but with an inner search for what he truly believed was right, beyond popular opinion or easy answers.
2. **Values act as a compass through chaos.** In a nation torn by war and division, Lincoln's steadfast commitment to equality and justice gave him direction and purpose, enabling him to navigate impossible choices.
3. **Choosing values is an act of courage, not convenience.** Lincoln's principles cost him popularity, peace of mind, and eventually his life. But these values made his leadership authentic and transformative.
4. **Consistency in values builds trust and legacy.** Lincoln's life shows how living according to deeply held principles—even amid complexity and conflict—creates lasting impact far beyond one lifetime.
5. **Freedom without direction is drift; values turn liberty into meaningful action.** Liberty is not just the absence of constraints, but the presence of guiding lights that orient every decision and define who you become.

3 CHOOSING PROGRESS OVER PERFECTION

The Step That Builds the Path

Imagine a sculptor staring at a block of marble, chisel in hand, paralyzed. He has studied the masters, measured the stone, envisioned the final form down to the smallest detail. But he cannot bring himself to make the first strike. Why? Because the first mark might not be perfect. Because once the stone is touched, it cannot be untouched.

This fear—the fear of imperfection—holds many of us hostage in modern life. We become thinkers without execution, planners without projects, learners without lived experience. We have replaced action with endless calibration, obsessed with getting it exactly right before we begin. But in doing so, we forfeit the single most essential ingredient of progress: movement.

The Myth of the Perfect Start

Perfection is a mirage that moves farther away the closer we get. It tricks us into believing that once we've read enough books, watched enough tutorials, or arranged our schedules just right, the moment of readiness will arrive. But readiness is not a static condition we reach—it is a state we grow into through action.

Modern life amplifies this paralysis. Social media bombards us with curated highlight reels of perfect bodies, perfect homes, perfect routines, perfect businesses. We rarely see the hundreds of attempts, the failed versions, the doubt-ridden nights that preceded the glossy outcome. As a result, our internal standards become inflated and unrealistic. We believe we must get it right the first time, or not at all.

This perfectionism is not a sign of high standards—it is often a sophisticated form of fear. We are afraid of looking foolish. Of being judged. Of discovering that we are not as talented as we hoped. So we stall, disguising inaction as preparation. We call it "being careful" or "waiting for the right time," but deep down, we are simply afraid to be seen failing.

The Stagnation of Untested Potential

The cost of this perfectionism is not just delayed projects or missed opportunities. It is the slow erosion of confidence and identity. When we wait too long to act, our sense of agency withers. We begin to doubt our own momentum. The idea that we might be someone who creates, builds, or leads begins to fade. We live in our heads, and life becomes theory instead of practice.

People who delay starting because they want to "get it right" end up stuck in a loop:

- They don't act because they fear failing.
- Because they don't act, they don't grow.

- Because they don't grow, their fears remain.

The antidote is not more thinking. It is movement. It is the humble, imperfect step forward.

Progress is Built on Feedback

Every artist, athlete, scientist, and innovator throughout history has progressed not by getting it right the first time, but by responding to feedback. Leonardo da Vinci's notebooks are filled with experiments that didn't work. Marie Curie's lab was full of dangerous trial and error. Thomas Edison famously said, "I have not failed. I've just found 10,000 ways that won't work."

The scientific method itself—arguably the most powerful engine of human knowledge—is based not on certainty, but on *falsifiability*, *iteration*, and *refinement*. A hypothesis is formed, tested, and adjusted. This is the only known way to produce real understanding in a complex and unpredictable world.

And so it is with life. The only way to find out what works for you— what business, partner, vocation, or philosophy is yours—is to test, reflect, adjust, and repeat. No amount of pre-analysis can replace the knowledge that comes from lived feedback. Thinking prepares us. But only action transforms us.

The Courage to Look Incomplete

One of the most difficult acts in a perfection-obsessed culture is to show up before you're ready. To speak while still learning. To publish while still unsure. To launch while still imperfect. But that is precisely what leads to growth. Every great writer has cringed at their early drafts. Every speaker has stumbled through awkward first talks. Every builder has demolished a failed prototype.

And here's the paradox: the willingness to look imperfect is what allows you to become excellent. The people we admire—musicians, leaders, thinkers—did not arrive polished. They became so because they gave themselves permission to be *in process* in front of the world.

Progress requires vulnerability. It means letting go of control over how others see you. It means accepting that mistakes will be made and criticisms will come. But it also means that you are alive in your becoming. That you are shaping something, learning something, becoming something. And that is infinitely more powerful than staying safely invisible.

The Progress Path Is the Only Path

There is no perfect version of your life waiting to be unlocked with the right algorithm. There is only the version you create, one step at a time, through choices made in good faith. These choices will sometimes be flawed. But they will be *yours*—and they will teach you what no abstract pondering ever could.

The truth is that you cannot steer a parked car. Movement, even uncertain movement, gives you leverage to change direction. Once you are in motion, feedback becomes your compass. The world begins to respond. You learn what excites you, what drains you, what you're willing to suffer for. You stop living in the land of potential and begin shaping the terrain of reality.

From Chaos to Craft

What begins as chaos—messy drafts, awkward conversations, clumsy attempts—over time becomes craft. Repetition builds skill. Reflection builds insight. Failure builds resilience. If you do not act because you fear imperfection, you rob yourself of the very process that leads to mastery.

Perfection is static. Progress is dynamic. Choose dynamism.

The Cost of Waiting

The longer you wait for perfection, the harder it becomes to begin. Like a muscle unused, your capacity to risk, to create, to act—atrophies. What begins as discernment turns into delay. What starts as caution becomes self-doubt. Time, once abundant, becomes an enemy.

You do not avoid risk by waiting. You increase it—because you forfeit the chance to learn while you still have time. And when you finally do act, the world may have changed. The door may have closed. The opportunity may have shifted. The only truly irrecoverable mistake is not acting at all.

The Philosophy of the First Step

There is a kind of spiritual clarity that comes when we give up the need to be perfect. When we choose instead to be honest, to move, to build as we go. Each step we take, no matter how small or flawed, is a declaration: I am here. I am willing. I am becoming.

The path does not appear before you. It is created by your footsteps. Every time you act, you mark the ground with intention. You give shape to a life.

Choose Progress

This is your invitation: let go of the illusion that you must be flawless before beginning. Let go of the idea that you can think your way to certainty. Embrace the truth that your life will be built through action, refined through feedback, and defined by the choices you dare to make.

The step builds the path. Take it.

Case Study: Thomas Edison (1847–1931)
The Relentless Tinkerer Who Refused to Wait for Perfection

Case Study: Thomas Edison (1847–1931)
The Relentless Tinkerer Who Refused to Wait for Perfection

Thomas Edison is often remembered as the genius who "invented the light bulb." But the truth is far more illuminating—and far more relevant to the idea of choosing progress over perfection. Edison's greatness was not born from a single moment of brilliance. It was forged in the fires of relentless trial and error, of small steps forward, of thousands of failures embraced as necessary progress.

Edison did not wait for the perfect idea, the perfect timing, or the perfect circumstances. He acted. He experimented. He failed publicly and repeatedly. But he moved forward constantly. In doing so, he became one of the most prolific inventors in history, holding over 1,000 patents in the United States alone and countless more internationally.

This is not just the story of invention. It is the story of a mindset—a mindset that offers a counterweight to our perfectionist paralysis today.

The Illusion of the Lightning Bolt

Popular culture often paints invention as a kind of divine spark—a eureka moment that arrives in a flash and solves everything at once. Edison shattered this myth through his methods.

His most famous quote is also his most misunderstood:

"Genius is one percent inspiration and ninety-nine percent perspiration."

That wasn't false modesty. It was a prescription. Edison knew that innovation—and life itself—was not about waiting for the perfect idea, but about refining imperfect ones. He understood that the path to success was paved with countless experiments, many of which would fail. But each one would teach.

For Edison, failure wasn't an obstacle. It was a *tool*.

The Light Bulb: Not One Invention, But Thousands of Decisions

When Edison set out to create a practical, affordable electric light, the concept already existed. Arc lamps had been used since the early 1800s, but they were expensive, short-lived, and dangerous. Dozens of inventors before Edison had tried—and failed—to solve the same problem.

But while others failed and stopped, Edison failed and *iterated*.

Between 1878 and 1880, he and his team tested over **6,000 different materials** for the filament. Cotton, linen, bamboo, wood splinters, metals, and even human hair. Thousands of prototypes were built. Every variable—filament thickness, vacuum pressure, electrical resistance— was adjusted and logged. Some tests worked for seconds. Others lasted minutes. Most simply failed.

To outsiders, this looked like madness or waste. To perfectionists, it seemed inefficient.

To Edison, it was *progress*.

When criticized for failing thousands of times, he replied:

"I have not failed. I've just found 10,000 ways that won't work."

In other words: progress is not what you arrive at. It is what you *move through*.

The Lab as a Theatre of Trial

Edison's Menlo Park laboratory in New Jersey—often dubbed "The Invention Factory"—was not a showroom of polished prototypes. It was a symphony of trial and error. There were no sterile presentations. There were loud arguments, bursts of enthusiasm, midnight rebuilds, and daily disappointments. But there was *movement*, always.

He structured his team not around control, but around *experimentation*. Dozens of assistants and researchers were expected to try things before perfecting them. Edison often told his staff not to "think about being right," but to *test what happens*. They were not solving problems in theory—they were building pathways through failure.

It was a radical departure from the perfectionist mindset.

This environment also had ripple effects. Menlo Park became a birthplace of industrial research methodology: constant iteration, rapid prototyping, and shared failure as collaborative progress.

Today, this approach echoes in modern tech development—especially in startup culture's embrace of the "minimum viable product" (MVP). It is Edison's legacy in action.

Not Waiting for Perfect Timing

Edison's decision to enter the electric lighting market came at a time of immense uncertainty. Gas lighting dominated cities. Electricity was dangerous and poorly understood. The infrastructure was nonexistent. Financial backers were skeptical.

A perfectionist would have waited for the market to mature, for safer conditions, for better technology. Edison charged forward.

He not only created the light bulb—he helped build the *entire system* needed to deliver it. That meant inventing generators, switches, and meters. It meant designing the first power stations. It meant persuading city officials and bankers. It meant countless new problems to solve, none of which had perfect solutions.

Perfection would have paralyzed him. But Edison understood that a *working version today* beats a flawless version *never begun*.

The Long Tail of Feedback

One of Edison's overlooked strengths was his ability to learn from everything—especially from what didn't work. He kept meticulous records. Every experiment was documented. Every failure became data. This was not just emotional resilience—it was a *system of learning.*

When an experiment failed, Edison didn't blame the tools or the team. He asked what new information it revealed. He understood that reality is the ultimate feedback loop—and that progress only comes to those who *risk engaging* with it.

Too many people today treat feedback as judgment. Edison treated it as *fuel.*

Perfection as the Enemy of Good Work

Had Edison waited for certainty, the world might have waited decades longer for electrification. But more importantly, *he* would have become someone different. Not the prolific inventor. Not the restless thinker. But a man known for big plans, and few results.

Edison's life is proof that **the willingness to be wrong in public** is more powerful than being right in secret.

He never claimed his inventions were flawless. In fact, he often admitted they were crude. But they worked, they evolved, and they opened doors for others to improve them.

The Legacy of Imperfect Progress

Today, Edison is credited with inventions that shaped the modern world: the phonograph, motion picture camera, electric grid systems, and of course, the incandescent light bulb. But his most important legacy is not any one device.

It is this: **Progress beats perfection. Always.**

Edison's life is a masterclass in starting before you're ready, persisting through failure, and learning faster than you fear. He didn't just invent tools. He lived a philosophy.

Lessons for the Perfectionist Age

In an era obsessed with instant success and polished presentation, Edison offers a radical example:

- You don't need the best plan to begin—just a next step.
- Failure is not the opposite of success; it is the *process* of success.
- Ideas without action remain nothing more than possibility.
- Perfectionism may protect your ego, but it kills your momentum.

Edison didn't wait to feel qualified. He qualified himself by doing.

You can too.

Here are **5 key takeaways** from the case study on *Thomas Edison* in Chapter 3: **Choosing Progress Over Perfection — The Step That Builds the Path**:

1. Progress Comes from Action, Not Planning

Edison didn't wait for the perfect idea or ideal conditions. He acted, tested, and iterated. Perfectionists stay stuck in planning mode, but builders make imperfect progress and refine along the way.

2. Failure Is Data, Not Defeat

Edison redefined failure as a tool for learning. Each failed experiment was a step forward in understanding. He didn't fear mistakes—he recorded them, studied them, and used them as fuel.

3. Perfection Is the Enemy of Innovation

The pursuit of perfection often delays or prevents real creation. Edison's light bulb wasn't perfect—it was good enough to launch a revolution. Done and improvable beats perfect and imaginary.

4. Start Before You're Ready

Edison tackled unsolved, risky problems without waiting for expertise or approval. He built the electric light system without anyone having done it before. Progress favors the bold, not the prepared.

5. You Become Through Doing

Edison became "Edison" not through vision alone, but through relentless doing. His identity as an inventor was shaped through thousands of small, imperfect actions—not through waiting for clarity or

4 THE PARADOX OF FREEDOM THROUGH FORM

The Gift of the Gate: How Constraints Liberate

In the mythology of modern life, freedom is often portrayed as the absence of boundaries—a wide-open sky, an empty calendar, a blank canvas. We associate freedom with limitlessness, imagining that the more options we have and the fewer rules we must follow, the more liberated we are.

But there is a deeper truth, one that artists, engineers, leaders, and builders throughout history have all discovered in their own way: **true freedom is not found in the absence of constraint, but in choosing the right constraints.**

This is the paradox of freedom through form: **the structure we resist is often the very thing that sets us free.**

The Myth of the Infinite Horizon

We've been sold a vision of freedom as boundless choice. In this view, every boundary is a threat. Rules are oppressive. Deadlines are stifling. Budgets are burdensome. Schedules are cages. This is the gospel of the frictionless life: do what you want, when you want, without limits.

But those who have lived with total freedom—whether in artistic fields, academia, or even utopian experiments—know how quickly boundlessness turns into aimlessness. When nothing is demanded of us, nothing gets done. When no direction is set, no path is followed. And when there are no stakes, there is no urgency.

Too much freedom does not expand us. It dulls us.

Freedom Without Form Becomes Drift

Consider the tenured academic who no longer faces pressure to publish or teach. Or the artist with unlimited time and funding. Or the early retiree with no financial needs, no obligations, and no schedule. Many such individuals imagine they'll finally create their magnum opus. But for many, time stretches out like an ocean with no wind—vast, flat, and strangely lifeless.

Without constraint, motivation decays. The human mind craves friction to push against. Deadlines, resource limits, competing demands—these shape our focus and provoke ingenuity. Without them, we drift.

The Liberating Power of Limits

Now flip the script. Imagine the same artist, but with only three colors and one day to paint. Imagine the writer given just one sentence to build a story. The designer tasked with creating a product using only recycled materials. The engineer solving a power problem with only $100 in budget.

Constraints seem like walls—but they are actually tools. **They sharpen focus, force clarity, and ignite creativity.**

In fact, most great innovations were not born from abundance, but from necessity.

- The Apollo 13 team's life-saving fix was crafted with a sock, duct tape, and plastic bags.
- The haiku's rigid 5-7-5 structure has inspired centuries of poetic brilliance.
- Startups often outperform larger corporations not despite limited resources, but because of them—they must solve problems fast and cheap.

Constraint doesn't kill creativity. It defines it.

The Form That Frees

Look at the violin. Four strings, limited range. And yet in the hands of a master, it can express a universe of emotion. The form—the tuning, the fingerboard, the bow—isn't a limitation. It's a vocabulary. It gives shape to possibility.

Look at language. If every person made up their own grammar, we wouldn't have communication—we'd have chaos. Grammar doesn't limit our freedom of speech. It makes speech possible. The structure is the vehicle for meaning.

Or take the idea of time: a 24-hour day. It feels restrictive, but this daily boundary helps us rest, recover, plan, and create rhythm. Imagine if each day were unbounded and time had no shape. Could we function, let alone flourish?

Structure is not the enemy of freedom. It is its scaffold.

Why Deadlines Motivate, Not Destroy

Many people resist deadlines, seeing them as stressful or oppressive. But deadlines are not just pressure points—they're launchpads.

- They **create urgency**, forcing us to focus on what matters most.
- They **eliminate perfectionism**, demanding completion instead of endless polishing.
- They **drive progress**, by breaking the future into achievable intervals.

Ask any writer who's ever met a publication deadline, any entrepreneur before a product launch, or any student cramming before an exam—deadlines get results.

Paradoxically, **without deadlines, we often produce nothing. With** them, we produce our best.

Constraints as Clarifiers of Vision

Consider the architectural marvels built in tight urban spaces. The best designs emerge not from open fields, but from working around zoning codes, light restrictions, and density regulations. These "limits" force clarity.

Or consider military strategy: generals rarely have ideal conditions. Victory often comes from making the most of uneven terrain, bad weather, or limited troops. It's not what you have—it's how you work with what you're given.

Constraints reveal character. They test resolve, invite creativity, and force trade-offs that reveal what truly matters.

The Psychological Comfort of Boundaries

Humans don't thrive in chaos. Psychologically, we crave rhythm, orientation, and meaning. Boundaries give us those things. This is why people follow routines, build habits, and appreciate rituals. Even the most "free-spirited" among us find deep grounding in form.

Too many choices? We crave a short list. Too much time? We schedule a break. Too much money? We create a budget. Too many ideas? We pick a theme.

Form provides focus. And focus unlocks flow.

True Freedom Is Disciplined Freedom

There is a difference between the freedom of a leaf in the wind, blown in every direction, and the freedom of a skilled dancer on stage. The leaf is directionless. The dancer has spent years practicing within a form— ballet, tango, hip hop—and now moves with grace and power.

That's not restriction. That's mastery.

Discipline is not the opposite of freedom. It is its foundation. The disciplined creator, thinker, or leader is free not because they do anything—but because they've chosen a path and committed to it fully.

Constraint as Commitment

In relationships, careers, and life paths, constraints are often the beginning of depth. A marriage vow limits romantic freedom—but deepens emotional intimacy. A chosen field limits other careers—but builds mastery. A startup founder gives up stability—but gains creative ownership.

Every meaningful life is shaped by chosen limits. We do not become great by leaving every door open. We become great by closing some— and walking fully through others.

A Life Without Walls Is a Life Without Shape

Freedom is not the erasure of form, but its intentional design. The gate you build—not the void beyond it—is what makes movement meaningful.

So don't fear the limits. Design them. Welcome them. Use them.

- Choose deadlines.
- Set boundaries.
- Work within form.
- Embrace scarcity.

Because **the gift of the gate is not in what it blocks, but in what it focuses.**

The Call to Constraint

You are not made smaller by boundaries. You are made sharper. You are not less free because of form. You are more powerful within it.

So the next time you resist structure, ask yourself: is this resistance really about freedom? Or is it about fear?

And then ask: what structure, what constraint, what chosen gate could actually set you free to build something that matters?

Freedom through form is not a contradiction. It is a choice. And it is one of the most powerful choices you can make.

Case Study: Ludwig van Beethoven (1770–1827)
How Embracing the Limitations Fueled Creativity and Mastery

Case Study: Ludwig van Beethoven (1770–1827)
How Embracing the Limitations Fueled Creativity and Mastery

In the late 18th century, Europe was changing. The Enlightenment had lit intellectual fires across the continent. Revolutions stirred in France and America. Empires rose and trembled. And in a modest town in Bonn, within the Holy Roman Empire, a boy was born into a family of musicians—a boy who would one day shatter every convention of music while hearing nothing at all.

His name was Ludwig van Beethoven.

The Burden and Blessing of Early Promise

From a young age, Beethoven was told he was special—sometimes gently, sometimes with brutal insistence. His father, Johann, hoped to mold him into a prodigy to rival Mozart. He forced long hours of practice, often waking the boy at night to rehearse. Music was not just talent; it was expectation. Even at age seven, when Beethoven performed publicly for the first time, he carried not just the burden of his father's ambitions, but the weight of an entire tradition.

And he did not disappoint. By his teens, Beethoven had become a virtuoso pianist and an accomplished composer. His early works sparkled with influence from Haydn and Mozart, yet hinted at something more volatile, more defiant. In his playing, there was both precision and storm.

By 22, Beethoven moved to Vienna—the epicenter of European music. He studied with Haydn and gained patronage from aristocrats. He was bold, proud, temperamental, and endlessly talented. Doors opened for him. He was free to choose his path, and the path promised greatness.

Until the one thing a musician cannot lose began to slip away.

The Rising Shadow: Deafness and Isolation

At first, it was subtle. A ringing in the ears. Difficulty hearing high notes. Beethoven, in his late twenties, dismissed it as temporary. But the symptoms worsened.

By 30, he was suffering from progressive hearing loss. By 35, he could barely hear conversation. By his 40s, he was functionally deaf.

For a composer, it was not just a tragedy—it was a cosmic joke. The gift that defined him was being swallowed by silence.

His affliction wasn't only physical; it was existential. Without hearing, could he still be a musician? Could he perform? Teach? Converse? Belong?

The freedom of his early life—the admiration, the salon concerts, the friendships—was replaced by isolation. He withdrew from public performance. He avoided social gatherings, unable to follow dialogue. He wrote anguished letters. In the famous *Heiligenstadt Testament* (1802), he confessed suicidal despair.

And yet—he did not end his life.

Instead, he made a decision that would change music forever.

The Turning Point: Choosing to Create Within Constraint

Beethoven did something extraordinary. He accepted the loss.

But he did not surrender to it.

He resolved that if he could no longer hear, he would compose music with his inner ear. He knew the timbre of instruments, the rules of harmony, the structure of form. He could imagine sound, even if he could not hear it.

And in the silence, a new kind of music emerged.

Without the distractions of performance or conversation, Beethoven plunged deeper into composition. And as his physical world narrowed, his creative world exploded.

His work became more experimental, more emotional, more structurally daring. He broke the clean lines of Classical form. He expanded sonatas, distorted tempos, smashed conventional resolutions. His symphonies became landscapes—dense, philosophical, transcendent.

And he did all this in near-total silence.

Constraint as Catalyst: The Innovation of the Middle and Late Periods

Had Beethoven retained his hearing, he may have continued as a brilliant Classical composer. But it was deafness that drove him beyond imitation into innovation.

His **Third Symphony**, *Eroica*, was twice the length of a typical symphony and broke every rule of form. It was loud, unpredictable, and filled with fury and grandeur.

The **Fifth Symphony** gave us four of the most famous notes in music history—short-short-short-long—a rhythmic motif born of tension, as if fate itself were knocking.

The **Ninth Symphony**, written when he was completely deaf, included a full choir for the first time in a symphony. It ends not with despair, but with an ecstatic *Ode to Joy*, celebrating universal brotherhood.

Even the **Late String Quartets**, inscrutable in their time, used unusual keys, dissonant harmonies, and shifting tempos that would not be understood until the modernist era. These works weren't just ahead of their time—they shattered the idea of time in music.

None of this would have been possible without his deafness. It was the ultimate gate. And Beethoven used it not as a wall, but as a lens—distilling his work into its most essential, most daring form.

The Discipline Behind the Genius

It is tempting to see Beethoven as a divine madman, scribbling furiously, conjuring symphonies from the ether. But his process was deeply disciplined.

He carried sketchbooks everywhere, obsessively reworking phrases, testing harmonies, refining structure. He studied counterpoint, internalized fugues, built musical architecture with the precision of an engineer.

He was not chasing inspiration; he was *building it*.

This was a man who understood that greatness is not freedom from limits—it is excellence *within* them. He did not wait for perfect conditions. He composed while ill, alone, broke, and cut off from the one sense his craft required.

He turned a constraint into a crucible—and emerged with fire.

Legacy: Constraint as a Source of Immortality

Today, Beethoven is not remembered merely as a great composer. He is remembered as a turning point—a bridge between Classical order and Romantic passion. He made music not to please salons or follow tradition, but to speak truth, to wrestle with fate, to uplift the human soul.

And that truth was forged in limitation.

Beethoven could not hear applause. He could not enjoy the sound of his own masterpieces. Yet he kept composing, because he believed in something beyond comfort: the power of discipline, of purpose, of beauty shaped by boundary.

His constraint became his canvas. His silence became his stage.

And from that silence came some of the most profound sound the world has ever known.

Here are **five key takeaways** from the case study of Ludwig van Beethoven and how constraint fuelled his creativity and mastery:

1. Limitations Do Not Diminish Potential—They Refine It

Beethoven's deafness, while tragic, forced him to rely on his internal mastery of music rather than external validation or convention. What could have ended his career instead concentrated his genius. His constraint distilled rather than diluted his creativity.

2. Acceptance of Reality Unlocks Creative Power

The turning point in Beethoven's life wasn't when he lost his hearing—but when he stopped resisting the loss. By embracing the reality of his condition, he freed himself to explore what was still possible, rather than mourning what was no longer available.

3. True Innovation Emerges Within Boundaries

It was precisely because of Beethoven's deafness—and the isolation it imposed—that he moved beyond the predictable boundaries of Classical music. The constraints on his senses expanded the boundaries of the art form itself, pushing music into new emotional and structural territory.

4. Discipline is the Engine Behind Genius

Despite romantic myths, Beethoven's brilliance was not born from chaos or madness. It came from relentless structure: sketchbooks, revisions, deep study, and methodical refinement. Constraint wasn't just something he endured—it was the scaffolding for his most daring work.

5. Legacy is Built Not in Ease, But in Struggle

Beethoven didn't compose for applause—he couldn't even hear it. He created because he believed in something greater than his own comfort: the transcendent power of art, the dignity of perseverance, and the possibility that beauty could emerge from silence. His immortal legacy was forged not despite constraint, but because of it.

5 THE ANCHOR IN A DRIFTING WORLD

The Sacred Act of Commitment

The Fog of the Unmoored

Imagine standing on a boat in the middle of a vast, endless sea. The sky is overcast, the wind shifts restlessly, and the currents tug in every direction. There is no map, no harbor in sight—only the whispered echo of distant lands. You have oars. You have sails. You even have time. But without a direction, you drift.

That's what life becomes without commitment. A long drift. A restless wandering that exhausts but never fulfills.

In a world saturated with options and always-on distraction, many have mistaken indecision for intelligence and flexibility for freedom. We've been trained to think that keeping our options open is a form of wisdom—that the refusal to choose is a mark of prudence. But over time, we discover a bitter truth:

The refusal to commit is not a strategy—it is a surrender.

The Pitfalls of Non-Commitment

To remain uncommitted is to place yourself in a perpetual waiting room. Time ticks by. Life moves around you. Others build, stumble, love, learn. And you? You research. You ponder. You delay. You craft ever more refined excuses cloaked in the language of "readiness" and "discernment."

But readiness is a lie. Life rarely offers perfect clarity before you act. It offers a window—and a whisper: *Begin.*

And if you do not begin, time will.

The Stoics put it plainly: **"If a man knows not to which port he sails, no wind is favorable."** — *Seneca*.

There is no wind that helps the drifter. No current serves the one who drifts aimlessly. The currents of time are powerful, but only if you fix your sail and steer. Otherwise, they simply carry you further from the shores of your potential.

1. Drifting Leads to Dissolution

Without commitment, the self begins to dissolve. When you are perpetually "exploring," you spread yourself thin. Interests are dabbled in, not mastered. Friendships remain shallow. Projects begin but do not end. The soul, like unshaped clay, dries out from exposure and neglect.

People forget that identity is not something you find—it's something you form. And you form it through sustained effort in a direction. Without commitment, you never become someone—you remain everyone. A thousand selves never lived.

2. The Illusion of Freedom

Non-commitment often masquerades as freedom. But freedom

without purpose is emptiness. It's freedom like a man who owns every book but reads none. Who visits every country but touches no community. Who dates endlessly but loves no one. The horizon expands, but your soul shrinks.

Freedom is not the ability to go anywhere—it's the power to go somewhere deeply. Commitment does not limit you. It liberates you from triviality. It gives your energy a container and your life a spine.

3. Time Doesn't Wait

Uncommitted people often assume they can start "later"—when things are calmer, clearer, easier. But time is not static. Every day of waiting is a day of erosion. Relationships fade. Skills atrophy. Momentum vanishes. You do not preserve possibility by postponing commitment—you consume it.

What's worse, the longer you drift, the harder it becomes to anchor. The body forgets how to row. The soul forgets what it wanted.

You cannot shape a legacy in theory. You must build it in action.

The Transformative Power of Commitment

If drifting is decay, commitment is creation.

To commit is to step into sacred territory. It is the moment when potential becomes reality—not all at once, but through the slow, steady accumulation of choice and discipline. It is the act of saying, "This matters. I will build it." And in that moment, the fog begins to lift.

1. Commitment Creates Identity

When you commit to something—be it a vocation, a relationship, a principle—you give yourself a home. You anchor your energy and attention. The self begins to take shape. Your days acquire structure. Your values crystallize in context. You are no longer floating—you are becoming.

Commitment is the forge of character.

2. Constraints Clarify Action

Paradoxically, commitment doesn't restrict your possibilities—it enhances them. When you limit your scope, you amplify your depth. Deadlines focus you. Relationships deepen you. Responsibility strengthens you. The very constraints people fear are what unlock their power.

Consider the violinist: her creativity does not flourish because she plays *every* note, but because she plays *specific* ones with mastery. The bow becomes her boundary—and her liberation.

3. Commitment Makes Progress Visible

One of the most demoralizing aspects of modern life is the absence of visible progress. When you dabble endlessly, you never finish anything. But when you commit, you begin to *stack* achievements. A body of work emerges. Skills accumulate. Relationships deepen.

Reputation builds. You begin to see the shape of your life—not in abstract dreams, but in lived reality.

This is how confidence grows—not from self-help slogans, but from *witnessing* your own consistency.

The Courage to Bind Yourself

To commit is an act of bravery. It means risking regret. It means facing failure. It means relinquishing the illusion that you can be everything, everywhere, to everyone.

But the risk is worth it—because only by choosing can you create.

The samurai swore to their path. The artist married their medium. The parent, the teacher, the builder, the founder—all of them stepped off the shifting sand into something firm. Not perfect. Not permanent. But *real.*

And that reality gave shape to their souls.

Commitment is Sacred

In a culture allergic to permanence, commitment has become radical. We are told to "keep our options open," to "hedge our bets." But meaning demands sacrifice. There is no masterpiece without surrender. No love without loyalty. No purpose without prioritization.

To commit is not to lose freedom. It is to *aim* freedom. To carve meaning from possibility. To say: "This is what I choose. And in choosing it, I become more."

The Anchoring Act

So what, then, is commitment?

It is the anchor you drop to claim your place in the sea of existence. It is the vow you make—not just to the work, or the person, or the cause—but to your own becoming.

It is how you build a life that leaves a trace, a memory, a legacy.

You don't have to get it all right. You don't have to find the one perfect thing. You only have to *choose* something worth staying for— and then stay.

Commit. Not because it guarantees success.

Commit because it guarantees direction.

Because it converts drifting into discipline.

And because it reminds you that this life—this short, sacred life—is not something to sample endlessly.

It is something to *shape.*

The Path Among the Maze

If life is a maze, then commitment is the footstep that turns a wall into a hallway. It is what distinguishes the wanderer from the builder, the dreamer from the maker.

You are not here to float.
You are here to *forge.*
And the forge begins with this sacred word:

Yes.

Yes, I will stay.
Yes, I will try again.
Yes, I will face the fear of missing out, and choose to be fully present here.
Yes, I will build—not in theory, but in time.

And that "Yes"—spoken not once, but daily—becomes your anchor.

Case Study: Marie Curie (1867–1934)
The Radiance of Resolve — A Life Forged by Commitment

Case Study: Marie Curie (1867–1934)
The Radiance of Resolve — A Life Forged by Commitment

The girl was born in Warsaw, in a time and place where science was a man's pursuit, and a Polish woman was expected to serve, not to search. The country itself was fractured, its sovereignty denied by imperial partitions. The Russian Empire ruled Warsaw with iron resolve, censoring thought, punishing defiance, and limiting education—especially for women. But from the earliest days, *Maria Sklodowska* was not content with the roles laid out for her. She was quiet, observant, intensely intelligent. Her father, a teacher of mathematics and physics, surrounded the home with instruments of inquiry. She read Newton in her teens. She memorized lectures she could not attend. The world gave her boundaries; she responded by seeking the infinite.

Her path, from the beginning, was steep.

Leaving the Familiar

Formal education in the sciences was denied to women in Russian-ruled Poland. But Curie would not be denied by institutions. With her sister, she joined the clandestine "Flying University"—an underground network of professors and students who defied the regime's restrictions on Polish and female intellectual life.

The lectures were secret. The labs were improvised. But the hunger for knowledge was real.

Unable to afford university abroad, she worked as a governess for years, sending her meager earnings to support her sister's medical education in Paris. The cost of her commitment was not theoretical; it was measured in lonely winters, in class envy, in long days teaching others' children while her own brilliance waited untrained.

But finally, at age 24, the door opened.

Crossing into the Unknown

In 1891, she arrived in Paris. The city of lights was also the city of minds. At the Sorbonne, she studied physics and mathematics with a ferocity bordering on asceticism. She was poor—often hungry, always cold. She studied by day and by night. She collapsed from malnutrition but did not stop.

Other students noticed her silence, her focus. She wasn't there for social games or for prestige. She had come to learn—and then to push the boundaries of what could be known.

It was in this place of intensity and solitude that she met Pierre Curie.

Alliances and Shared Vows

Pierre Curie was an accomplished physicist in his own right—known for his work on magnetism and piezoelectricity—but also a kindred spirit. When he met Marie, he recognized a mind equal to his own and a devotion that matched, perhaps exceeded, his own scientific idealism.

They married, not in grand fashion, but with simple conviction. She wore a dark blue dress so it could be used in the lab. Their partnership was one of intellectual alignment as much as love. Their home was a laboratory. Their family included voltmeters and radioactive samples.

Together, they set their sights on a mystery at the edge of the known world.

The Descent into the Invisible

Wilhelm Röntgen had discovered X-rays. Henri Becquerel had observed strange emissions from uranium salts. Something invisible, yet powerful, was being released from matter itself. The Curies resolved to investigate. They coined the term *radioactivity*.

Working in a leaky wooden shed behind the school, with no ventilation and little funding, the couple processed *tons* of pitchblende—a uranium-rich ore—to isolate the unknown elements within. The labor was grueling. She stirred cauldrons of boiling material herself. Her hands were blistered. She wore no protective equipment. There were no models to follow—only a frontier to chart.

They discovered *polonium*—named for her beloved Poland—and then *radium*, an element so potent it glowed in the dark. The work brought fatigue, burns, and illness. They did not yet understand the dangers of radiation. But they understood that discovery required sacrifice.

Pierre wrote: "She is an extraordinary woman. She works far more than I do."

Recognition, Loss, and Solitude

In 1903, the Nobel Prize in Physics was awarded to Pierre and Marie Curie (and Becquerel). It was a revolutionary moment—the first time a woman had received such an honor. But Marie was not interested in celebrity. Fame distracted from purpose. She returned to her work.

Then, in 1906, tragedy struck.

Pierre Curie, crossing a street in the rain, was struck by a horse-drawn cart and killed instantly. He was only 46. The loss shattered Marie's world. Her partner in mind and soul was gone. She was left with two daughters, a nation of doubters, and the ghosts of radiation that had already begun to haunt her body.

She could have stopped. She could have retreated into grief. No one would have blamed her.

But commitment is not merely emotional. It is directional. It is what you become when you can no longer fall back.

Reclaiming the Work

Marie took over Pierre's teaching position at the Sorbonne, becoming the first female professor in the university's history. Her lectures, delivered in the same hall where she once sat as an invisible student, were precise, passionate, and austere. She spoke little of herself. She spoke often of radium.

In 1911, she won a second Nobel Prize—this time in Chemistry—for her discovery of polonium and radium, and for isolating pure radium metal. No one, before or since, has received Nobel Prizes in two different sciences. Yet even then, her integrity was tested. That same year, French newspapers leaked letters revealing her brief, post-widowhood affair with physicist Paul Langevin. She was called a foreign seductress, a home-wrecker. Protesters gathered outside her house. The Nobel committee urged her to decline the award to avoid scandal.

She refused.

"I believe there is no connection between my scientific work and the facts of private life," she wrote.

She accepted the prize. She returned to the lab. The work went on.

Building for Others

Her final years were marked not only by discovery, but by legacy. During World War I, she developed mobile X-ray units—called "Little Curies"—and trained nurses to use them to treat soldiers on the front. She raised funds for research institutes. She trained the next generation of scientists, including her daughter Irène, who would also win a Nobel Prize. Her own health, however, deteriorated. Years of radiation exposure—unknown, unchecked—had damaged her organs. She suffered from fatigue, cataracts, and recurring illnesses. But she never complained. She never slowed. The fire that burned within her had become her marrow.

In 1934, at the age of 66, she died of aplastic anemia—a condition likely caused by prolonged radiation exposure.

Legacy: A Life That Chose Its Light

Marie Curie did not live a balanced life. She lived a chosen one. She did not chase every passion, or weigh every option. She chose one thing and gave it everything. Her commitment was not to fame, or safety, or comfort—but to truth.

She refused to patent radium. She believed science should be free. She turned down riches, but not rigor. She endured criticism, poverty, sexism, heartbreak. Yet she never surrendered the anchor of her work.

Today, her notebooks are still radioactive. She changed not only physics and chemistry, but the role of women in science—and the very idea of what is possible when one life is wholly dedicated to the pursuit of knowledge.

Marie Curie did not drift. She steered. She sailed into darkness to pull from it a light no one had ever seen. And when the world tried to unmoor her—through loss, through scandal, through fatigue—she held fast.

Her life is not a monument to brilliance. It is a testament to resolve.

Here are **5 key takeaways** from the case study of **Marie Curie** and her unwavering commitment:

1. Commitment Requires Sacrifice — But It Builds Legacy

Marie Curie gave up comfort, social approval, and even her health in pursuit of discovery. What she gained was something far greater: a scientific legacy that has inspired generations. True commitment demands something from you—but gives something back that endures.

2. Constraints Are Not Cages, They Are Crucibles

Denied formal education in Poland and dismissed in French academic circles, Curie turned limitations into fuel. Her lack of access sharpened her focus. Her adversity refined her will. She didn't wait for ideal conditions—she created breakthroughs within imperfect ones.

3. A Singular Focus Can Be More Powerful Than a Thousand Options

Rather than trying to "do everything," Curie chose one purpose and let it define her. This focused life allowed for depth, innovation, and mastery. Her example shows that clarity of purpose can generate exponential impact.

4. Integrity Sustains Commitment When the World Doesn't

When scandal, grief, and public doubt threatened to derail her, Curie didn't fold. She refused to separate her private dignity from her public mission. Commitment is not just perseverance—it's staying true to what matters when it would be easier to quit.

5. A Committed Life Leaves a Trail for Others

Marie Curie didn't just break ground in science—she carved a path for women, immigrants, and underdogs in every field. The life of someone who commits fully is not just an achievement. It becomes a *map* others can

6 EVERY OPTION HAS A PRICE

The Bazaar of Souls

Step into any ancient marketplace and you'll feel it—an atmosphere alive with color, sound, and movement. It is not just commerce—it is drama. Voices calling, bartering, promising. Every object glimmering with potential. Every path branching into unknown consequence. This is the human experience: not the lack of options, but their overwhelming abundance. And in this grand bazaar, what you choose to buy is less important than what you are willing to give up.

The most important truths of life aren't free—they're forged. And every identity you take on has a cost. Every conviction you adopt will be tested. To declare a value is to beckon the storm that will measure it. To stand for something is to invite everything that stands against it.

The Identity of Values — And the Weight They Bring

When you say, "I am honest," life will give you chances to lie to protect yourself. When you say, "I am brave," it will place you in moments of fear. When you say, "I value freedom," you will be tempted with comfort and conformity. This is the paradox of values—they don't just describe you, they summon the trials that define you.

To choose integrity is to be given moments of secrecy. To choose compassion is to face betrayal. To choose courage is to wrestle with anxiety. Every value you truly own invites not ease, but exposure. And that is exactly how it becomes real.

You do not become a person of character by picking a word and wearing it like a badge. You become one when that word costs you something—and you pay it.

This is the price of meaning in the Bazaar of Souls: every virtue must be bought, and it is paid for in struggle.

Chaos as the Cost of Clarity

We often think clarity brings peace. But the truth is harder. Choosing a path doesn't simplify life—it throws into sharp relief everything you've refused. Clarity doesn't quiet the world; it stirs it. It doesn't end chaos; it organizes it around your purpose.

And that organization is costly.

The moment you declare a commitment—to truth, to freedom, to love—you become a magnet for chaos. Not because the world punishes ideals, but because it tests them. Like heat to metal, the trial burns away the impurities, forging strength or shattering illusion.

Ask those who've stood for anything real—revolutionaries, reformers, healers, builders. They will tell you: the test of your values is not abstract. It is heartbreakingly, terrifyingly concrete. It's lost friendships, rejected promotions, sleepless nights, physical exhaustion, and aching self-doubt.

But it is also what separates the tourist from the pilgrim. The dilettante from the craftsman. The dreamer from the builder.

Opportunity Cost in the Age of Infinite Options

We are told we can be anything. And it's true—but only if we're willing to not be everything else. Every great life comes with great opportunity cost. You want to be a parent? You may sacrifice spontaneity. You want to be an entrepreneur? Comfort will not be your friend. You want to be a warrior for truth? Get used to solitude.

There's a reason so few people build legacies. It's not because they're not talented—it's because they never choose which storm to weather.

The lie of modern life is that you can avoid loss by keeping your options open. But you don't escape loss that way—you just delay the meaning that could've come from commitment. Your time is not a renewable resource. Each year you stay uncommitted, your legacy shrinks.

The path of value is not the path of ease. But it is the path that leads somewhere solid. Somewhere future generations can stand.

Values That Build Legacies

Why do some names echo through centuries while others vanish in the dust? Because some people did more than exist—they stood. They chose a value and lived it so fully, so sacrificially, that it no longer belonged only to them. It became a foundation others could build on.

Think of Nelson Mandela, who chose forgiveness and reconciliation after 27 years in prison. Think of Malala Yousafzai, who chose education and courage in the face of death. Think of Václav Havel, who chose truth and dignity against the weight of a totalitarian regime. They paid dearly. But they left behind not just work—but *witness*.

Their legacies are not monuments to success—they are lighthouses of meaning.

The Currency of Legacy

Every decision costs. But not every cost is wasted. Some become the currency of a legacy. Your sacrifice today can be someone else's strength tomorrow.

The values you uphold, when tested and not abandoned, become the seeds of culture. They become stories passed down, blueprints for courage, frameworks for future builders.

And they begin now—not when you're ready, not when life is easy—but the moment you choose.

Choose your value. Let it define you. Let it test you. Let it cost you.

Because in the Bazaar of Souls, you will not be remembered for what you browsed. You will be remembered for what you *bought with your life*.

Case Study: Rosa Parks (1913–2005)
The Cost of Courage in the Bazaar of Souls

Case Study: Rosa Parks (1913–2005)
The Cost of Courage in the Bazaar of Souls

There are moments in history that appear small on the surface—quiet, even uneventful. A woman takes a seat. A bus rolls through town. Nothing explodes. No armies march. Yet within that quiet act lies the tectonic shift of an entire world.

Rosa Parks' refusal to give up her seat on a segregated Montgomery bus in 1955 was one such moment. But to understand the depth of its power, and the magnitude of its cost, we must step back—not just to the day she said "no," but to the crucible in which that "no" was forged. Her choice wasn't sudden. It was cultivated. And it came with a price.

The Early Fire: Growing Up Under Oppression

Rosa Louise McCauley was born in Tuskegee, Alabama, in 1913—a place and time where racial segregation was more than law; it was atmosphere. Black children were taught to lower their eyes. Schools were separate and unequal. Justice, when it came, came unequally, if at all.

Her grandfather, who sat on the porch with a shotgun during Klan marches, was her first teacher in defiance. Her mother taught her dignity through education, and Rosa learned to resist not through outrage, but through endurance. From her earliest days, she knew the weight of the world she had been born into. But she also learned something else: how to carry that weight with purpose.

As a young woman, she worked as a seamstress and cared for her family. But her mind never rested. She read. She listened. And quietly, she studied the rules of a society that sought to erase her, not to obey them, but to understand precisely how to bend—and one day break—them.

The Calling: Choosing a Value Over a Life of Ease

By the 1940s, Parks became active in the Montgomery chapter of the NAACP, working with people like E.D. Nixon to document acts of racial violence and injustice. She investigated cases of sexual assault and wrongful imprisonment. She wasn't just watching from the sidelines. She was preparing.

To choose dignity as your guiding value in a world of forced humiliation is not abstract philosophy. It is a call to suffer. It is a deliberate invitation to chaos.

She did not have wealth. She did not have institutional power. But she had the courage of someone who understood this simple truth: every option has a price. And she was ready to pay.

When she enrolled in the Highlander Folk School, a Tennessee training center for civil rights activists, she deepened her knowledge. She wasn't radicalized—she was refined. She saw how peaceful resistance could move systems that guns could not. She began to see that the future could be different—but only if people stood up and chose that future, no matter the personal cost.

The Crucible: A Simple Act with a Shattering Impact

December 1, 1955. Montgomery, Alabama.

Rosa Parks boarded a city bus after a day of work. She sat in the "colored" section, as the law required. When the white section filled up, the driver demanded she give up her seat.

It was not the first time this had happened—not for her, not for others. Black passengers were regularly asked to give up their seats, even forced off buses entirely. Rosa herself had once been thrown off a bus by the same driver for refusing to enter through the back.

But this time, she remained still.

She was not tired of walking, as she would later say. She was tired of giving in.

The consequences began immediately. She was arrested and fingerprinted. She lost her job. Her husband quit his job when his employer forbade him to talk about Rosa. They received threats. Their home became a target.

And yet, from that single act emerged the Montgomery Bus Boycott—a protest that would last 381 days. A movement was born, not in shouts but in silence, in walking, in waiting, in daily commitment to a principle larger than oneself. And Rosa, though never seeking the spotlight, became the symbol of that choice.

The Price: Isolation, Struggle, and the Weight of Legacy

It is easy, in retrospect, to romanticize what came next. Rosa Parks, hailed as a heroine, honored later in life with medals, memorials, and global praise. But in the years immediately after her arrest, she lived in hardship.

She and her husband relocated to Detroit. They struggled to find steady work. Even within the civil rights movement, she was sometimes sidelined—seen as a symbol rather than an active leader. The myth of Rosa Parks as a tired seamstress obscured the strategist, the activist, the woman who had spent years preparing for that moment of defiance.

The stand she took was not rewarded with ease. It was rewarded with burden. But she bore it because she had committed—not to fame, but to freedom. Not to comfort, but to conscience.

That is the price of choosing identity in the Bazaar of Souls. Once you stake your claim in the market of meaning, you become accountable to it. You are tested. You are weighed. And you often pay in silence.

The Legacy: A Light for Those Who Walk After

Rosa Parks did not act alone. But her decision became the fulcrum on which a national movement pivoted. Because she chose to sit, others chose to rise. The bus boycott propelled Martin Luther King Jr. into prominence. It led to a Supreme Court decision declaring segregation on public buses unconstitutional. And it helped galvanize a broader struggle that would reshape America.

And yet, her real legacy cannot be measured in legal victories or newspaper headlines. It is measured in the millions of quiet acts of courage her example inspired. In every person who decided to resist injustice not with rage but with resolve, Rosa Parks lives on.

Because she chose a value—dignity—and lived it fully, without compromise, others could find their own anchor in a drifting world.

Conclusion: Every Option Has a Price—And a Reward

Rosa Parks' story reminds us that the values we claim are not lifestyle decorations. They are commitments. And commitment has a cost.

In a world that tells you to go along, to survive, to stay quiet, to keep your head down, choosing to live your values is to walk into the storm willingly. It will shake you. It will strip things from you. It may leave you alone. But it will also make you.

And what it makes can outlast empires.

When you choose a value in the Bazaar of Souls, you purchase not ease, but meaning. Not applause, but resonance. Not safety, but immortality.

Rosa Parks paid the price. And because she did, we all inherited part of the reward.

Here are five takeaways from the case study of **Rosa Parks — The Cost of Courage in the Bazaar of Souls**:

1. **Choosing a Value Means Inviting a Test**
Rosa Parks didn't stumble into her stand by accident. She had long chosen the value of dignity and justice. But choosing a value isn't a private affair—it becomes a public commitment, and life will test whether you truly mean it. Her choice to remain seated wasn't just symbolic—it was the culmination of years of inner preparation to face external trials.

2. **The Price of Integrity Is Often Isolation**
After her arrest, Rosa faced economic hardship, social strain, and personal loss. She wasn't immediately celebrated—she was threatened, fired, and displaced. True commitment rarely wins immediate reward. It asks whether you're willing to stand by what you believe even when it costs you comfort, income, or approval.

3. **Legacy Is Built in Silence, Not Headlines**
Though her refusal ignited the Montgomery Bus Boycott, Rosa Parks did not live the life of a spotlight-seeker. Her influence grew from her quiet resolve. Real legacy is less about loud declarations and more about sustained moral courage—decisions made in the storm that ripple out for generations.

4. **A Single Act Anchored in Principle Can Move the World**
Parks' decision to sit down catalyzed a national civil rights movement. It's a testament to how a singular, grounded act—when backed by conviction—can reshape history. Every individual who dares to act in alignment with their values contributes to the architecture of freedom for others.

5. **The Bazaar of Souls Demands a Price—but Offers Immortality**
When you enter the "bazaar" of moral identity, you trade ease for meaning. Parks bought her place in history not with ambition, but with sacrifice. The world tested her choice, and she endured. In doing so, she became not just a participant in history, but a cornerstone of it.

7: THE HOLLOW CHASE OF THE HEDONIC TREADMILL

Pleasure's Mirage: When More Leaves Us Empty

We live in an age of abundance. Food, entertainment, connection, distraction—all of it just a tap or swipe away. We consume, scroll, snack, click, flirt, binge, and buy at a pace unthinkable even a generation ago. Every desire has a delivery system. Every impulse has a digital buffet waiting for it. And yet, with all this supposed freedom and pleasure, why are we more anxious, distracted, and unfulfilled than ever?

The answer lies in the very nature of unfiltered pleasure. Like drinking salt water, the more we consume, the thirstier we become. This is the heart of the hedonic treadmill: the endless pursuit of more, where each step forward takes us nowhere.

The Illusion of Lasting Satisfaction

The hedonic treadmill describes the psychological phenomenon where people quickly return to a baseline level of happiness despite positive or pleasurable changes in their lives. You get the raise, the new phone, the vacation, the dopamine hit from a viral post—and within days or weeks, it all feels normal again. The emotional high fades. Your appetite resets.

Pleasure has diminishing returns. It is a fleeting shadow that demands more of itself just to maintain the illusion. This isn't to say pleasure is bad—on the contrary, pleasure can be beautiful, necessary, and deeply human. But when pursued without reflection or responsibility, it becomes a trap, not a treasure.

Overindulgence and the Body

Take food, for instance. Evolutionarily, we were built to crave sugar, fat, and salt. These were rare, life-saving energy sources in the wild. Today, they're engineered into every processed snack, turned into a hyper-palatable cocktail that hijacks our biology. We no longer eat to live—we snack to stimulate. Obesity rates soar, metabolic diseases flourish, and our health declines not from starvation, but from surplus.

Overconsumption isn't about evil corporations or poor discipline alone—it's about the mismatch between ancient instincts and modern availability. But our responsibility is to recognize the mismatch and choose differently.

Information Gluttony

What food is to the stomach, information is to the mind. The digital age has created an all-you-can-eat buffet of opinions, news, images, and entertainment. We gorge on feeds, timelines, and alerts, believing that knowing more will help us feel more secure, more connected. Instead, it paralyzes us.

We become addicted to novelty, but allergic to depth. Our thoughts skim the surface. We mistake knowing for understanding, reacting for reasoning, and dopamine for truth.

There's a reason ancient traditions emphasized silence, contemplation, and fasting—not just for the body, but for the mind. Information without discernment is noise. To think clearly, we must filter ruthlessly.

Pleasure Without Purpose

Sex, too, has become a commodity in modern life. In the name of liberation, we've turned intimacy into transaction. Porn offers a facsimile of connection. Dating apps gamify desire. Sexuality, like all pleasures, has become another avenue for stimulation divorced from commitment or meaning.

Again, it's not the pleasure that corrupts—it's the absence of intention. Pleasure without purpose is like fire without a hearth. It may burn bright, but it leaves nothing behind but ash.

The Tyranny of Other People's Opinions

Even our self-worth has been outsourced. In a culture saturated by followers, likes, and shares, we begin to consume other people's approval as though it were nourishment. We define success not by what we build or believe, but by what others affirm.

Living for others' validation is the most insidious pleasure of all, because it dresses itself up as connection. But in reality, it fragments our identity. We become hollow avatars, curating ourselves for applause.

We must reclaim the right to judge our own path. No algorithm will save us. No influencer will give us peace. The only compass that works is the one we calibrate ourselves.

The Filter Is Responsibility

The common theme in all these modern excesses is the absence of a filter. Not a technological filter, but a moral one. A personal one. A conscious practice of saying: enough.

Pleasure must be tempered by purpose. Consumption by contribution. Stimulation by stillness.

And the filter? It can only come from within.

No one else is going to protect your mind, your body, your values. The market doesn't care if you drown in dopamine. The algorithm isn't designed to honor your soul. Only you can choose the standard by which you live.

Choosing Joy Over Stimulation

Pleasure is reactive. Joy is generative.

Pleasure happens to us. Joy flows from us.

When we create, serve, love, build, or grow, we generate joy. When we simply consume, we numb ourselves with pleasure. One feeds the ego; the other feeds the soul.

We must stop mistaking escape for engagement. Numbness for relief. Indulgence for freedom.

Building a Life That Lasts

The ultimate test of a life well-lived is not how much pleasure we felt in the moment, but how much meaning we carried through the storm.

Legacy is not built on sensation. It's built on sacrifice. And discipline. And a refusal to chase every flashing light.

When we step off the hedonic treadmill, we can begin to walk a real path—not one of endless loops, but of forward motion. Of focus. Of fire.

Of a life that counts.

And it begins when we look at all the pleasure the world offers and say: "I choose better."

Not more. Just better.

Not escape. But presence.

Not applause. But purpose.

Because in a world that sells you comfort, the real revolution is choosing meaning.

Case Study: Oscar Wilde (1854–1900)
The Price of Living for Applause — A Life of Brilliance and the
Shadows Beneath It

Case Study: Oscar Wilde (1854–1900)
The Price of Living for Applause — A Life of Brilliance and the Shadows Beneath It

The Alluring Prodigy

Born in Dublin in 1854 to an intellectually vibrant Anglo-Irish family, Wilde was the son of a celebrated surgeon and a poetess who styled herself a revolutionary. His home was a salon of ideas, a theatre of language. He learned early that words could enthral, that intellect could dazzle, and that to be admired was to wield a kind of power.

He absorbed the classics at Trinity College, then flourished at Oxford, where he cultivated his devotion to beauty, art, and paradox. Even as a student, Wilde became a public character—eccentric, witty, and provocatively different. He wore velvet jackets and lilies in his lapel. He mocked convention with such elegance that it could not help but be seduced.

But behind the aesthetic flair was a sharp, searching mind. Wilde absorbed the ideals of aestheticism: "art for art's sake," the idea that beauty required no justification. But this creed, while liberating, would later lead him down a path where truth could be dismissed if it interrupted pleasure—where restraint could be seen as an enemy of freedom.

The Meteoric Rise

London was Wilde's stage, and he played his role to perfection. His essays charmed the literati; his plays, such as *The Importance of Being Earnest* and *An Ideal Husband*, filled theaters. With biting wit and satirical brilliance, Wilde exposed the hypocrisies of Victorian society while remaining its darling. He was lionized and envied. Every room he entered seemed to brighten.

But the brilliance came at a cost. Wilde's success demanded constant performance. He became addicted to attention, to affirmation, to the applause of strangers. He crafted a persona of excess and nonchalance, finding his identity in public admiration. Privately, he indulged in affairs, luxury, and sensation—not in rebellion alone, but in a desperate pursuit to feel more, to stay afloat in the whirlpool of excess he'd created.

He called pleasure the "only thing worth having in life," and said, "Nothing succeeds like excess." But these quips masked a gnawing hunger that no amount of adoration or indulgence could satisfy. Like a man forever thirsty in salt water, he kept sipping.

The Turning Point

It wasn't Wilde's art that brought him down, but a relationship— intoxicating and ill-fated.

Lord Alfred Douglas, known as "Bosie," was a beautiful young aristocrat with whom Wilde became romantically entangled. Their relationship was tempestuous, decadent, and fraught with emotional volatility. Wilde, ever the aesthete, described Bosie as a living work of art. But Bosie was also manipulative and reckless, drawing Wilde further into the abyss of self-indulgence and defiance.

When Bosie's father, the Marquess of Queensberry, accused Wilde of "posing as a sodomite," Wilde—against the advice of friends—sued him for libel. It was a catastrophic misstep. The trial that followed uncovered Wilde's private life, exposing him to public shame. What had been a life of carefully choreographed performance was now torn apart under the merciless gaze of Victorian morality.

He was convicted of "gross indecency" and sentenced to two years of hard labour.

The Fall and the Silence

Prison broke Wilde—not just physically, but spiritually. Gone was the satin-draped wit and the glittering salons. He lived in solitude, silence, and physical pain. The body that once delighted in luxury grew frail. The mind that sparkled now turned inward, forced to confront the hollowness of the path he had walked.

In prison, he wrote *De Profundis*, a long, confessional letter that is perhaps his truest work. It is a meditation not on pleasure but on suffering, not on beauty but on meaning. He admitted, "I had been a spendthrift of genius...I forgot that every little action of the common day makes or unmakes character."

He no longer spoke of pleasure as salvation. He spoke of humility, of remorse, of the soul's slow work in darkness.

When he was released in 1897, Wilde was a shadow of his former self. He lived in exile in France under an assumed name, estranged from his family and most of his friends. He wrote little. He died three years later in a dingy hotel room, broke and alone.

The Hollow Pursuit

Wilde's life is often misread as a martyrdom of genius crushed by society's intolerance. There is truth in that—but it is not the whole truth.

Wilde was destroyed not just by the injustice of others, but by his own relentless pursuit of sensation over substance. He believed the highest good was to feel intensely, to provoke, to entertain, to bask in the moment. But moments pass. And when the applause fades, the self must still endure. The pleasures Wilde chased—luxury, lovers, fame—could not anchor him when the winds turned. His identity, so built on what others thought, had no core of its own. When stripped of adornment, he was left with questions he had long postponed.

Wilde's tragedy is not simply that he was punished, but that he did not commit to anything that could outlast the tides of fashion and flattery. He had the talent to build monuments of truth and beauty—but he built a house of mirrors instead.

Legacy: The Mirror and the Warning

And yet, even in his failure, Wilde teaches us.

His life warns against confusing charm with character, pleasure with purpose, applause with achievement. It asks us to look at the image we project into the world and ask: Is this truly me, or a mask shaped by what others want?

Wilde had every gift—language, intellect, imagination. What he lacked was a compass. And without that compass, his genius became a wandering light, dazzling but untethered.

He said, "I can resist everything except temptation." It was meant as a joke. But it became his epitaph.

Here are **5 takeaways** from the case study of Oscar Wilde in *The Hollow Chase of the Hedonic Treadmill: Pleasure's Mirage*:

---

1. Charm Can't Replace Character

Wilde mastered the art of impressing others, but not the discipline of shaping himself. Talent and wit can open doors, but only integrity can keep them open. A life built on performance without principle is a house of cards—beautiful, but unstable.

---

2. Pleasure Without Purpose Becomes a Trap

Wilde's pursuit of pleasure became compulsive, not liberating. When we make stimulation the goal—whether through attention, indulgence, or acclaim—we end up needing more and more for less and less fulfillment. The hedonic treadmill always promises joy but delivers emptiness.

---

3. Public Applause Can Drown Out the Inner Voice

Wilde became so attuned to external validation that he neglected his inner compass. He mistook the roar of the crowd for self-assurance. When we rely too heavily on others' admiration, we lose touch with our own convictions—and collapse when the cheers stop.

---

4. Suffering Can Clarify What Success Conceals

It was in prison, not in fame, that Wilde confronted the truth about himself. His letter *De Profundis* was a painful reckoning—but also a work of redemption. Sometimes, adversity reveals what comfort conceals: our need for depth, humility, and direction.

---

5. A Life of Substance Requires Restraint

Wilde had all the brilliance required to create timeless meaning, but he lacked the self-mastery to direct it toward lasting ends. True freedom isn't found in limitless indulgence—it's found in choosing what to say no to, so you can say yes to what matters.

8: FORGING THE SELF
THE BIRTHPLACE OF MEANING IN ACTION

"What we do is who we are becoming."
"You become what you give your attention to."
— Epictetus

The Shadow Between Idea and Impact

There is a silent cemetery in every mind—a graveyard of intentions never acted upon.

In it lie the dreams we dreamed but did not pursue, the talents we glimpsed but never honed, the kindnesses we meant to show, the projects we almost began. These unmanifested fragments form a haunting truth: that without action, all our thoughts, all our insights, all our best selves remain unborn.

The modern world does not suffer from a shortage of ideas. It suffers from an epidemic of *non-execution*. We consume books, podcasts, conversations, insights. We write notes, think deeply, post reflections, share theories. But how many of those sparks are forged into something solid, into a living fire?

Thoughts are seeds. But only *action* is the soil.

Without commitment to action, even the most profound revelation evaporates. It remains locked in the realm of potential—a wisp, not a world. Without execution, there is no self forged, no legacy formed, no impact made. A life well understood but poorly enacted is still a life unlived.

Action as Identity

People speak of "finding themselves" as though the self is some fossil buried beneath the sand. But identity is not found. It is *forged*.

We do not discover who we are through thought alone. We sculpt it, day by day, through what we *do*. Every choice, every act of persistence, every small creation chisels us into form. We do not become by dreaming—we become by building.

Action is where identity and meaning converge. It's in waking up early to write the book you keep imagining. It's in starting the business instead of endlessly researching it. It's in painting the canvas, publishing the essay, lifting the weight, making the call, taking the walk. Your habits are your biography. Your rituals are your religion. Your output is your offering.

Each executed action says: *I was here. I mattered. I tried.*

The Mirage of Infinite Preparation

Why do we wait so long to act?

Because preparation feels safe. It feels like movement. But endless preparation is the enemy of execution. It is procrastination with a prettier face.

You'll never feel fully ready. The stars will never fully align. No strategy is perfect until tested in the furnace of reality. Execution will always expose your vulnerabilities—but that's exactly the point. Action is feedback. It is friction that hones the blade. It is failure that teaches the hand to strike with precision.

The craftsman does not wait for perfect wood. She works with what she has and makes it better with her hands. Likewise, we must stop asking whether we are "ready." Instead, we must ask: *What is the smallest next step I can do with integrity right now?*

Then do it. Then repeat.

Comfort: The Great Delayer

Execution requires cost. And the first price it demands is the death of comfort.

It is easier to remain in the imagined version of ourselves—the writer who hasn't written, the entrepreneur with ideas but no customers, the friend who meant to reach out. These identities are painless because they are *fictional*. Execution collapses the fantasy and confronts us with our actual state.

The gym hurts. The blank page terrifies. The first cold email is humiliating. Building something worth doing always costs time, energy, ego, sleep, safety.

But that's precisely why it gives back so much more. Sacrifice is the price of transformation. What we trade in comfort, we receive in *clarity*—about our values, our voice, our limits, and our potential.

The furnace of action does not destroy the self. It reveals it.

Execution as Immortality

You will one day be gone. This is not a threat—it is a promise. What will remain?

Not your dreams. Not your unspoken thoughts. Not your good intentions. Only your actions will linger.

Your body of work is your real biography. Every act of generosity, every bridge you built, every poem you shared, every problem you helped solve—these become your echoes. These become the fingerprints you leave behind.

No one remembers da Vinci's plans. They remember the Mona Lisa. No one studies the notebooks of Beethoven's daydreams. They study the symphonies. No one is inspired by the sermon never spoken or the policy never enacted. We are moved only by what was *done*.

To build a life of meaning, we must create what didn't exist before us—and leave behind something that couldn't exist without us.

From Thinking to Building

There is a strange temptation in modern life to conflate *insight* with *integration*. We hear something wise, feel its truth, and mistake that emotion for transformation. But nothing has changed until we change what we do.

We have to break the loop of passive consumption. We must turn the inward into outward. The abstract into concrete. The spiritual into practical. Action is the only bridge between belief and becoming.

You do not become a writer by studying literature.
You become a writer by writing.
You do not become courageous by reading philosophy.
You become courageous by *acting while afraid*.
You do not become wise by hoarding insight.
You become wise by *living insight out loud*.

The Execution Mindset

To turn insight into execution, develop a new mental model: *Bias toward creation.*

Whenever you learn something new, ask:
→ What can I *do* with this?
→ What change in behavior does this require?
→ How can I build this into my work, relationships, or routines?
Then do it—imperfectly, publicly, often.
Create more than you consume. Publish more than you polish. Move forward more than you hesitate. Life rewards those who ship.

Conclusion: Legacy Is Built, Not Dreamed

In the end, the only way we know ourselves is through what we *have done*—and what we *are doing*. Our greatest act of meaning is not discovering the perfect identity. It is becoming someone worth being through our daily acts of courage, creativity, and commitment.

We must not die full of potential. We must die *empty*—because we poured everything we were into something greater than comfort, greater than distraction, greater than ourselves.

Execution is not the death of freedom. It is its birth. Because the only self that matters is the self we *forge*—in action.

"Don't explain your philosophy. Embody it."
— Epictetus

Case Study: Steve Jobs
The Alchemy of Action

Case Study: Steve Jobs
The Alchemy of Action

In a quiet garage in Los Altos, California, an odd but intensely curious young man began shaping the arc of his life with little more than vision, obsession, and an abiding discomfort with the ordinary. Steve Jobs didn't wait to be invited into greatness. He built the door himself—and kicked it open.

But that image of Jobs as a world-shaping force, the black-turtlenecked oracle on the Apple stage, was not born fully formed. It was forged—through fire, through failure, through ferocious decisions that demanded action far before perfection was in sight.

To understand the life of Steve Jobs is to see what happens when someone refuses to let thought die unborn—when ideas are not only envisioned but executed into existence with a radical sense of urgency and faith.

The First Spark

Steve was never content to merely learn what others knew. From an early age, he seemed tuned to a frequency the rest of the world couldn't hear. He wandered between calligraphy classes, acid trips, Eastern philosophies, and impromptu visits to engineers' workshops, absorbing ideas like kindling.

But vision alone was not what made Jobs Jobs. It was his *insistence* on acting on those visions. The founding of Apple wasn't the product of a five-year plan. It was a spontaneous act of courage, catalyzed by his friend Steve Wozniak's clever computer board and Jobs' refusal to let it be a curiosity that died in obscurity.

What they had was primitive. But Jobs saw a future that didn't yet exist: sleek personal computers in the hands of ordinary people. The dream was massive. The tools were small. But they built anyway.

Jobs made a decision that would define the rest of his life: **build first, refine later**. Action was everything. He sold his Volkswagen van. Wozniak sold his HP calculator. And with those humble sacrifices, Apple was born.

The Trial of Creation

The first products were assembled by hand. The resources were laughable. The deadlines were impossible. But Jobs pushed. Always. Harder than was reasonable. He demanded not just function, but beauty. He obsessed over packaging, fonts, startup sounds—details others found irrelevant, Jobs found sacred.

And with that mindset, Apple began to change the world.

But action carries its own price. As Apple grew, so did the complexity. Jobs' demanding perfectionism bred tension. His refusal to compromise alienated colleagues. His vision outpaced his leadership maturity. Eventually, the very company he helped birth rejected him.

He was fired.

The world saw it as a downfall. Jobs saw it—eventually—as *freedom*.

"I didn't see it then," he later said, "but it turned out that getting fired from Apple was the best thing that could have ever happened to me."

The exile became an anvil. It did not shatter him. It shaped him.

Exile and Reinvention

Jobs did not disappear into resentment or bitterness. He built.

He founded **NeXT**, a company dedicated to creating powerful workstations for higher education. Though the products never broke through commercially, the technology and design principles became foundational to Apple's future. Even his failures were investments in the road ahead.

He bought **Pixar**, a struggling graphics division from George Lucas, and nurtured it into the greatest animation studio in the world. He didn't know how to animate. But he knew how to demand excellence, how to push for emotional resonance, how to *make something happen*. And something did: *Toy Story*, a revolution in cinema, and an empire of storytelling.

Through the wilderness years, Jobs kept *doing*. Kept building. Kept evolving. He transformed from a brilliant tyrant to a focused creator. From a brash leader to a builder of culture.

By the time Apple came calling again, he was not just ready to return. He was ready to remake it in his image.

The Great Return

In 1997, Apple was floundering. The company that had once changed the world now stood on the brink of irrelevance.

Jobs re-entered not as a nostalgic founder, but as a *man on a mission*. He slashed product lines, restructured the company, and focused on *execution over everything*. No more scattered visions. No more endless experimentation. Just: **Build insanely great products. Deliver. Repeat.**

And he did.

In just a few years, Jobs and his team introduced the iMac, the iPod, iTunes, the iPhone, the iPad—each a juggernaut, each reshaping not just technology, but how humans live.

These weren't accidents of innovation. They were acts of relentless execution—vision *made real*. Each product began as an intuition, a sketch, a whisper of possibility—and was wrestled into form through Jobs' demand for coherence, simplicity, and soul.

Mortality and Meaning

Even as his health declined, Jobs did not stop. He designed the Apple Store. The iPhone 4. He planned Apple's future campus—every curve of the glass, every tree in the courtyard.

Why? Because for Jobs, *execution was immortality*. He once said:

"We're here to put a dent in the universe. Otherwise, why else even be here?"

That dent is not metaphor. It is literal. Because Jobs did more than think big—he *acted big*. And because of that, we live in a world he reshaped:

how we talk, how we listen to music, how we work, how we think about design, how we imagine the future.

Even his death was marked by creation. His final words to biographer Walter Isaacson weren't instructions about legacy or legacy management. They were a product roadmap. He was *still building.*

The Legacy of Action

Steve Jobs left behind no great philosophical treatises. No diaries of introspection. He left behind a trail of objects: tools, devices, experiences. Tangible echoes of a mind that refused to stay theoretical.

That is his greatest lesson.

Do not wait until the plan is perfect.
Do not let the vision rot inside you.
Do not let the comfort of imagination replace the courage of creation.

Build. Launch. Learn. Repeat.

Jobs did not become Steve Jobs through talent alone. He became who he was because he *refused* to stop executing. Because he *acted* in the face of doubt, resistance, failure, and fatigue. Because he believed the world could be remade—not through thought, but through *tangible, relentless, intentional action.*

He dreamed. He did. He changed everything.

.

Here are **five takeaways** from the case study of **Steve Jobs** for Chapter 8: *Forging the Self — The Birthplace of Meaning in Action.*

1. Ideas Alone Mean Nothing Without Execution

Jobs was never short on ideas—but what made him extraordinary was his relentless insistence on bringing those ideas into the world. A sketch is not a product. A vision is not a revolution. Action is the bridge between thought and transformation. Execution is what makes the invisible visible.

2. You Are What You Build

Steve Jobs didn't just "have" a career—he *forged* an identity through the work he committed to. Each project he delivered wasn't just a product; it was a sculpting of the self. Legacy isn't some abstract ideal. It's the body of work you leave behind—proof that you were here, that you *did something.*

3. Comfort Is the Enemy of Creation

Jobs thrived in discomfort. He was willing to be misunderstood, fired, doubted, and even disliked, if it meant honoring the creative process. Those who insist on comfort rarely create anything meaningful. The furnace of difficulty refines not only the product, but the person.

4. The World Doesn't Need Another Dreamer—It Needs Builders

Many dream. Few deliver. Jobs was obsessed with timelines, deadlines, launch dates. He turned abstract possibilities into real-world impact because he respected the discipline of shipping. In a world flooded with vague ambitions, his legacy is a monument to **deliberate, disciplined output**.

5. Action Is Immortality

Jobs' final years were not spent on nostalgia or rest. They were spent *building*—even knowing his time was short. Because he understood: when we create with intention, our work outlives us. He didn't just live his life. He *forged* it—one bold decision at a time. The question he leaves for all of us is simple: **What are you building that proves you were here**

9: FREEDOM THROUGH FOCUS

The Narrow Light That Illuminates All

There is a myth that freedom lies in having more choices. But for those who have truly changed the world—not merely existed within it— freedom was born not in options, but in focus. In saying *no* a thousand times. In drilling into the dark earth of an idea until something radiant emerged.

What separates the extraordinary from the average is rarely intelligence, luck, or charm. It is the brutal, unwavering commitment to go deeper than others are willing. To endure boredom, obscurity, discomfort, and ridicule long enough for truth to reveal itself.

The Light Comes Through the Narrow Gate

The mind, like light, becomes powerful when focused. A candle can be blown out by the wind. A laser can cut through steel. The difference is not more energy—it is more direction. So too with human potential. When we scatter our attention across the countless stimulations of modern life, we remain dim, flickering across surfaces but never penetrating them. Yet when we focus, when we choose one question and refuse to look away, we begin to gather something rarer than information: *insight*.

This insight—the sharpened intuition of a mind that has truly dwelled with an idea—is not a gift. It is not natural genius. It is not inherited. It is earned. And the price is high.

The True Cost of Depth

Depth does not come cheap. The pursuit of mastery has its own gravity—it demands isolation, obsession, sacrifice. It requires hours, years, sometimes decades of immersion. And it often begins in the wilderness of obscurity.

You will not be cheered on. You will not be applauded. No one throws parades for those who stay late after the lights have gone out, who keep showing up when motivation dies, who labor invisibly while others scroll and self-promote.

To reach depth, you must surrender breadth.

To create something timeless, you must temporarily abandon the present.

To see clearly, you may need to turn away from the crowd.

True focus means others will not understand. It means you might miss the parties, the praise, the ease of the ordinary path. You may be called obsessive. You may feel alone. But the irony is this: in that solitude, you will find what the distracted can never grasp—clarity.

Intuition: The Fruit of Devotion

Many speak of "intellectual intuition" as if it were magic—as if some minds are simply blessed with a sixth sense for pattern and truth. But intuition is not divine luck. It is the result of relentless attention.

It is the chess grandmaster who has stared at the board for decades, the artist who has painted until their brush becomes an extension of thought, the scientist who has asked the same question ten thousand different ways until an answer appears unannounced.

Their minds do not guess. Their minds *see*—because they have paid the price to see.

This kind of clarity cannot be downloaded. It cannot be fast-tracked. It can only be forged in the fire of sustained effort. It is built layer by layer until the structure of understanding is so sound, so embodied, that what looks like instinct is actually memory—compressed wisdom, ready for use.

The Discipline of Simplicity

The deepest thinkers do not make things more complex. They hammer at confusion until only the essential remains. They know that clarity is not a starting point—it is a reward. It is the summit that comes after the climb.

To simplify without dumbing down is an art that requires total immersion. Anyone can say something complicated. But to speak the truth with elegant precision? That is rare. That is earned.

It is not just what you know. It is what you can express, and more importantly, what you can *build*. And building—real building—requires focus sharp enough to shape raw potential into form.

The World's Distractions Are Not on Your Side

In the age of endless stimulation, the enemies of focus are many: algorithms designed to hijack your attention, opinions masquerading as truth, the cult of productivity that celebrates motion over meaning. The world will not protect your depth—it will erode it.

And no one else is going to draw the line for you. No one else is going to say: *This is enough distraction. This is what matters. This is what I will give my life to.*

Only you can do that.

And you must.

Because time is not waiting. And neither is your potential. The price of perpetual diversion is a life unlived. Not because you lacked talent, but because you lacked traction.

What Will You Build?

The question is not whether you are capable of greatness.

The question is whether you are willing to suffer for it.

Will you sit with your craft long enough to find its voice?

Will you ask one question so relentlessly that the universe must answer?

Will you let go of comfort in pursuit of clarity?

Because here's the quiet truth: the narrow light—the one that leads to brilliance—is available to all. But only a few ever walk its path. Not because they're better, but because they endure.
They endure distraction. They endure failure. They endure loneliness.
And from that endurance, something immortal is born.
So ask yourself now, and ask honestly:
What would you be capable of… if you gave yourself entirely to focus?
What world could you build if you stopped scattering and started sculpting?
Are you willing to pay the price of depth… so you can shine like no one else?
Because if you are—
Then there is nothing… absolutely nothing… that can stop you.

Case Study: Nikola Tesla
The Man Who Harnessed Lightning

Case Study: Nikola Tesla
The Man Who Harnessed Lightning

There are lives that flash across the world like a spark—brief, brilliant, and gone before we've fully understood what we saw. Nikola Tesla was one of those sparks. A man who gave the world its electrical skeleton, yet lived much of his life in the dark. Not because he failed—but because he saw farther than those around him could comprehend.

He was not chasing fame. He was not chasing fortune. He was chasing truth. And he would pay any price to catch it.

The Call of the Invisible World

Born in 1856 in Smiljan, a small village in the Austrian Empire (modern-day Croatia), Tesla was not an ordinary child. Even as a boy, he possessed a rare ability to visualize complex mechanisms in his mind with photographic precision. He would later call this his "inner world," a place where he could run experiments and imagine inventions without touching pen or paper. But the outside world didn't understand that gift. He was ridiculed, doubted, and sometimes feared. To others, he was odd. To Tesla, the real world was merely a sketchpad for the designs already etched into his mind. From a young age, Tesla knew he was meant to dedicate his life to something vast—something electric. And so he left his homeland, carrying nothing but dreams that glowed brighter than the lights he would later invent.

Trials in the Land of Opportunity

He arrived in New York in 1884 with four cents in his pocket, a bundle of notes, and a letter of introduction to Thomas Edison. The letter described him as a man of genius. But in a country fueled by industry and profit, genius meant little if it didn't produce money.

Tesla found work with Edison, who initially promised him a hefty bonus for improving the company's inefficient dynamos. Tesla, working tirelessly, reengineered the system from the ground up. When he finished, Edison allegedly laughed off the promised reward as a joke. Tesla quit on the spot. This was the first of many betrayals. The world he had entered did not reward vision—it rewarded advantage. But Tesla refused to play that game. He would compete not through politics or public relations, but through focus and innovation.

The Forge of Obsession

Tesla did not invent electricity. But he saw how it could move. He understood its rhythm, its flow, its music. While Edison backed the direct current (DC) model, Tesla pursued alternating current (AC)—a system that could carry power farther, faster, and with far less waste.

To champion AC was to stand against the era's titans. The media turned on him. Edison's allies spread fear about his technology. Public demonstrations involved electrocuting animals to paint AC as dangerous. Investors grew wary. Tesla's name became both feared and misunderstood. But Tesla kept building. Kept refining. Kept sacrificing.

His days were consumed with experimentation. His nights with restless vision. He worked so intensely he often forgot to eat. He walked the city to think, sometimes twelve miles at a time, running calculations in his head.

He developed compulsive routines to maintain mental clarity. And when setbacks came—and they always did—he turned inward, sharpening his focus like a blade.

He was not in it for recognition. He once said, "I do not care that they stole my idea… I care that they don't have any of their own." He believed the idea mattered more than the name attached to it.

Lightning Strikes the Earth

In 1893, at the World's Columbian Exposition in Chicago, Tesla finally had a chance to show the world what he saw. Powered by his alternating current, the fair dazzled the world with electric light. For many visitors, it was the first time they had seen a building illuminated at night.

It was more than a technical victory—it was a cultural one. Tesla's focus, his refusal to abandon the AC dream despite opposition, lit up the future. The "War of Currents" had been brutal. But AC had won. And Tesla, the misunderstood visionary, had transformed the world's infrastructure.

He didn't stop there.

He dreamed of wireless communication years before anyone believed it possible. He conceived of the smartphone, the internet, and wireless power—decades before the world caught up. He developed the Tesla coil, which became a foundation for radio and x-ray technologies. His patents laid the groundwork for everything from radar to robotics.

But these dreams came at a terrible cost.

The Descent Into Isolation

Despite his victories, Tesla's life did not grow easier. He had little interest in managing money, and his obsession with ideas often alienated patrons. Some of his grandest visions—like the Wardenclyffe Tower, meant to provide free wireless energy—frightened investors who saw no way to profit from them.

He was betrayed again. Abandoned by financiers. Ridiculed in the press. The tower was dismantled. His laboratory was seized. His dreams were shelved.

Yet still he did not stop thinking. Alone in his hotel room, walking the streets of New York, feeding the pigeons he'd come to love, Tesla never ceased inventing. He lived in modest obscurity, drifting toward poverty. And yet his mind stayed lit, a private generator still humming with possibility.

He once said, "The present is theirs; the future, for which I really worked, is mine."

And he was right.

The Return of the Light

Tesla died in 1943, alone and nearly forgotten. But today, his name is a symbol not only of innovation—but of integrity. Of vision. Of the cost of seeing farther than others.

We live in the world he dreamed of. A world powered by currents he championed, connected by technologies he foretold. Though the world did not honor him in his time, the future he built continues to illuminate our lives.

And what allowed him to build that future was not ease. Not charisma. Not luck.

It was *focus.*

Relentless. Sacrificial. Absolute.

Tesla endured obscurity, poverty, betrayal, and public ridicule because he believed in something bigger than himself. He surrendered comfort so that the world might inherit light.

Are You Willing?

Tesla's life is not merely a story of genius. It is a challenge.

Are you willing to focus like he did?

Are you willing to be misunderstood, mocked, and ignored for the sake of something true?

Are you willing to give up comfort to build something real—something that lasts beyond you?

Because freedom, real freedom, does not come from having it easy.

It comes from knowing what you will give everything for—and doing it.

That is the narrow light.

And those who walk it change the world.

Here are **5 detailed takeaway points** from the case study on **Nikola Tesla**, tied to the chapter *Freedom Through Focus — The Narrow Light That Illuminates All*:

---

1. Depth Demands Isolation — Great Focus Comes at a Personal Cost

Tesla's life reminds us that high achievement often requires stepping away from the noise of the world. His focus bordered on monastic—forsaking wealth, fame, and social ease in order to pursue ideas that lived only in his mind. The question for each of us is not just *what* we want to build, but *what we're willing to give up* to build it.

---

2. Vision Without Execution is Daydreaming — He Made Ideas Real

Tesla didn't just theorize; he *built*. His mental clarity was matched by a compulsion to manifest what he saw in his imagination. Focus is not passive—it's the active hammering of intuition into structure. Without execution, even the most brilliant ideas die in silence.

---

3. Obsession Over Distraction — The World Will Try to Steal Your Attention

In a time when others chased profit and popularity, Tesla kept his eyes on his principles. His story is a warning: the world will offer applause for mediocrity and riches for compromise. Staying focused means being constantly tested by offers that demand your soul in exchange for comfort.

---

4. True Focus is Purpose-Driven — Not Just Productivity, But Meaning

Tesla wasn't focused for the sake of being productive—he was focused because he *believed*. He had a mission. And that's what carried him through setbacks, betrayal, and poverty. Focus without meaning is discipline without fire. What gives you the right to endure discomfort is the clarity of your *why*.

---

5. The Future Belongs to the Focused — The Narrow Light Illuminates All

Tesla died in obscurity. But today, we live in the reality he envisioned. His work proves that those who walk the narrow path—who master the one thing they were born to do—cast long shadows across time. Focus is not about the moment; it's about eternity. Are you willing to light that torch?

10: THE ENDLESS ASCENT

Becoming Through the Climb

There is no mountaintop. No final resting place for those who build. No moment where it all finally makes sense and the world stops asking more of you. For those who truly embrace the path of creation, the summit is not the end—it is the beginning of the next climb.

This is the truth few tell you: mastery is not a destination, but a discipline. It is not granted once and for all. It must be earned again and again through relentless engagement with reality. And the ones who build legacies, not just monuments, are those who understand that the work is never over.

They build not because they expect a final reward, but because they have seen how fleeting the rewards are. They climb not because the climb is easy, but because not climbing would be worse—a surrender to inertia, to the slow death of potential.

The Builders Who Never Stop

Look closely at the world's most lasting achievements and you'll often find behind them not a moment of brilliance, but a person who refused to stop building. These are the ones who, once they reach the top of one mountain, don't settle in. They look out, see the range stretching far beyond, and begin the next ascent.

These are the systems thinkers. The integrators. The builders of builders. Once they understand their own strengths and limitations, they don't just work harder—they work smarter. They design structures. They gather minds sharper than their own. They build ecosystems where insight and execution compound across time.

Their secret isn't genius. It's endurance.

Elon Musk, for all his polarizing qualities, did not stop at building one company. SpaceX, Tesla, Neuralink, and more all arose not from a restless ego but from a repeated pattern: learn, test, build, launch, scale, and then ask what next.

Reed Hastings, after co-founding Netflix, didn't cling to DVD rental as the pinnacle. He cannibalized his own model, went digital, bet on streaming, and later on original content—each decision a calculated risk born not from fear of change but an embrace of it.

This kind of sustained ascent is not about burnout or masochism. It's about **living in the rhythm of growth**. Knowing that the game is never over, and that's what makes it worth playing.

Systems Over Spurts

To ascend endlessly, you must shift from heroics to systems. Heroics can get you started—pull an all-nighter, launch the product, fix the bug. But they cannot sustain you.

The ones who endure are those who turn their insights into processes, their breakthroughs into principles. They document what works. They reflect on what fails. They build teams not just for tasks, but for thinking. They develop rituals that replenish rather than drain.

They no longer look for one-off wins. They look for **flywheels**: self-sustaining cycles of effort and reward that grow with time.

Knowing Your Limits, Then Expanding Them

Endless ascent is not blind ambition. It is informed humility.

Builders who last are those who become intimate with their own limits. They know when to push and when to pause. When to bring in help and when to dig deeper. They are not threatened by smarter people; they seek them out. They are not ashamed of failure; they mine it for insight.

This humility allows them to take **calculated risks**. They test assumptions, iterate rapidly, and adapt without ego. Because they are not trying to be right once. They are trying to evolve endlessly.

And in doing so, they shed the illusion that there is an "it" to reach. No single project, title, company, or amount of money can replace the joy of playing the long game, well.

The Climb is the Point

When you begin your journey, you may think the goal is to "arrive." To finally have a title. To finally have respect. To finally build the company. To finally make the money.

But if you are fortunate enough to reach those early peaks, you will realize something disorienting: **Arrival is a mirage.**

The satisfaction fades. The struggle returns. The world keeps moving. And so must you.

But here is the secret joy: the climb becomes your calling.

Each ascent strengthens your legs. Each fall teaches resilience. Each view broadens your perspective.

You learn to love the climb not because it gets easier, but because it makes you more.

The Cost of the Climb

This way of life is not without sacrifice. To keep climbing, you must give things up:

- Comfort
- Certainty
- Predictability
- Pleasing others
- The illusion of control

You will outgrow relationships. Outpace your old definitions of success. You will face doubt, boredom, fatigue, and envy.

And yet, you will also find something rare:

- Momentum
- Mastery
- Mission
- Meaning

You will realize that **the cost of not climbing is higher than the cost of the climb.**

The Invitation

You are not asked to climb forever out of obligation. You are invited to climb endlessly as a choice.

To become a builder not just of things, but of self. To become a thinker not just of ideas, but of systems. To become a leader not just of people, but of vision.

And most of all, to become someone who plays the infinite game of growth without needing applause, guarantee, or rest.

Because the work itself becomes its own reward.

So the question is not whether the climb ends. The question is:

Are you willing to keep climbing?

Case Study: Warren Buffett (1930–)
The Relentless Climb of the Oracle of Omaha

94

Case Study: Warren Buffett (1930–)
The Relentless Climb of the Oracle of Omaha

In a small midwestern town named Omaha, Nebraska, a boy was born into modest comfort, with nothing in his surroundings that suggested greatness—except for an extraordinary obsession. By the age of seven, Warren Buffett had read every book on finance and investing in the local library. While other children were losing themselves in games and fantasies, he was memorizing stock tables and running mathematical experiments in his head.

He was not driven by wealth for wealth's sake. What drew him was the puzzle—the thrill of deciphering patterns, of testing his logic against the impersonal currents of the market. His childhood was not filled with pageantry, but it was lit with an inner fire: a desire to *understand* and a need to *apply*.

But understanding, as Buffett would learn, is never static. It deepens only through the trials of time.

The First Ascent: Discipline Over Dazzle

At 11, Buffett bought his first stock—three shares of Cities Service Preferred. The stock dropped, then rose. He sold it at a small profit, only to watch it soar higher later. It wasn't just a beginner's lesson—it was the start of a philosophy. Patience matters more than impulse. Discipline beats emotion.

By the time he entered college, Buffett had turned his paper route money into thousands of dollars. He was precise, frugal, and already treating each dollar as an investment soldier sent out to bring back reinforcements.

In 1950, he studied under Benjamin Graham at Columbia Business School. Graham's doctrine of *value investing*—buying undervalued stocks with a margin of safety—felt like divine truth to Buffett. But even as a disciple, Buffett refused to be a blind follower. He tested ideas. He questioned. He adapted.

His early career saw modest gains. He returned to Omaha and started his own partnerships. He read voraciously, investing with almost monk-like asceticism. When others followed trends, he followed fundamentals. When others chased speed, he chased value.

But every philosophy, no matter how sound, faces its reckoning.

The Storm: The Crisis of Identity

As the 1960s turned to the 1970s, Buffett's value investing principles were put to the test. The market became manic. Growth stocks surged. Speculation replaced prudence. The investing world that once rewarded method now chased momentum.

Buffett faced his first great moment of internal reckoning. The style that built his identity—the slow, patient method—was now seen as obsolete. Friends urged him to adapt, to become more aggressive, to play the game differently.

But Buffett chose retreat over reinvention. In 1969, he shut down his investment partnership. In his letter to investors, he admitted he could no longer find opportunities that met his standards. He would not chase fashion. He would not compromise process for profit.

Many thought him finished.

But that retreat was not surrender. It was recalibration.

Buffett had set his sights on something greater than yearly returns. He wasn't interested in just making money. He wanted to *build* something that would last beyond him. That vision led him to Berkshire Hathaway.

The Foundry of Permanence

Berkshire was a failing textile company. By traditional standards, it made no sense as a foundation. But Buffett wasn't interested in the fabric. He was interested in the *structure*. He would use Berkshire as a holding company, a platform through which he could acquire enduring businesses.

This shift marked a new stage of ascent—not just as an investor but as a builder.

He bought insurance companies like GEICO, whose cash flows he could reinvest. He bought See's Candies, a small but wonderfully run business with pricing power. Over decades, he added railroads, energy, and media.

Each acquisition was chosen not because it was trendy, but because it was durable. He sought *moats*—advantages that protected a business long-term. He sought *integrity*—people he could trust to run them. And above all, he practiced *focus*—sticking to what he understood, saying no to 99 out of 100 ideas.

This philosophy wasn't exciting. But it was *exponential*. Buffett's fortune grew slowly, then suddenly.

The Quiet High Ground

In time, the same world that once dismissed him came to revere him.

He was now known as the "Oracle of Omaha." Investors hung on his every word. Presidents asked for his counsel. His annual shareholder letters became masterpieces of clarity and candor.

And yet, Buffett remained unchanged. He lived in the same modest home he bought in 1958. He drove himself to work. He ate McDonald's for breakfast. His thrill didn't come from status, but from solving problems—and from teaching others to do the same.

He believed wealth was not to be worshipped but stewarded. That's why, in 2006, he pledged to give away the vast majority of his fortune, beginning with a $30 billion donation to the Gates Foundation.

Buffett understood that the climb isn't complete when you reach a peak. Every summit only reveals a broader horizon. And so, in his 90s, he still wakes up to play the game—not for glory, but for the joy of mastery.

The Climb Never Ends

Buffett's life is not just a tale of compounding capital. It is a testament to compounding *conviction*.

He faced a world of noise and chose clarity. He faced temptations of ego and chose humility. He faced countless forks in the road and chose the one that aligned with his values—even when it was the harder path.

His focus, his willpower, his insistence on understanding before acting—these were not traits he was born with. They were forged, sharpened, and tested across decades.

And the legacy he builds is not just measured in billions, but in the ideas, habits, and mindsets he has left for generations of thinkers, builders, and doers.

Are You Willing to Climb?

The world is full of shortcuts, of peaks climbed quickly and forgotten just as fast.

But Buffett's life asks us a harder question:

Are you willing to play the long game?

Are you willing to endure boredom, doubt, and mockery for the sake of something real?

Are you willing to spend a lifetime mastering your craft, saying no to the noise, and yes to the truth?

Because if you are—if you can focus like he did, build like he did, and give like he did—then the climb won't just be yours.

It will be a path others follow long after you're gone.

Here are **5 key takeaways** from the case study of **Warren Buffett — The Relentless Climb of the Oracle of Omaha**:

1. Conviction Must Outlast the Crowd

Buffett's greatest strength wasn't just financial acumen—it was the unshakable conviction to follow his principles when everyone else veered away. Whether the world mocked or misunderstood him, he remained focused on his long-term vision. True clarity often looks like foolishness in the short term.

2. Build Systems, Not Moments

Instead of chasing one-time wins or trendy opportunities, Buffett created enduring systems—a holding company, a philosophy of investing, and a legacy of partnerships. Builders think in decades, not in quarters.

3. Simplicity Requires Mastery

Buffett turned complexity into clarity. His ability to simplify came not from naïveté but from deep understanding. Intellectual humility and curiosity—combined with a ruthless filter—allowed him to stay focused on what mattered.

4. The Peak Is Just Another Starting Point

Every time Buffett reached a new height, he used it as a foundation to climb again. He never "retired" mentally or rested on his laurels. For those truly committed to growth, there is no final destination—only the next mountain.

5. Legacy Is a Choice, Not an Accident

Buffett didn't just accumulate wealth—he intentionally designed how it would be used, given, and remembered. By building with purpose and giving with vision, he ensured that his impact would ripple far beyond his own lifetime.

ABOUT THE AUTHOR

Sharath K. Bhaskaran is a leadership strategist, writer, and lifelong student of liberty-centered living. As the author of *Lead with Liberty: How to Lead in a Multicultural World*, which helps leaders around the globe navigate the complex intersections of freedom, culture, and collaboration with clarity and principle. His writing offers a bridge between timeless values and modern realities—blending classical liberal thought with actionable tools for today's decision-makers.

Sharath is also the founder of **Liberty Quill**, a news aggregation platform that distills global developments through the lens of individual liberty, voluntary cooperation, and civic responsibility. Whether addressing institutional leadership or personal growth, his work is guided by a single conviction: that meaningful progress begins with empowered individuals acting freely and responsibly.

With a background spanning organizational leadership, cross-cultural strategy, and civic engagement, Sharath's ideas resonate with readers who are navigating a world of overwhelming choices, shifting norms, and competing narratives. He draws inspiration from thinkers as varied as **Leonardo da Vinci**, **Carl Jung**, **Frederick Douglass**, and **Marie Curie**—those who forged paths not by following the crowd, but by listening to their conscience and committing to the long climb.

When he's not writing or advising principled teams, Sharath is usually exploring decentralized systems, engaging with emerging philosophical ideas, or connecting with builders and reformers across cultures—people who are not waiting for permission, but forging better futures one deliberate choice at a time.